HOLY DISRUPTOR

HOLY DISRUPTOR

Shattering the Shiny Facade by
Getting Louder with the Truth

AMY DUGGAR KING

WITH SUSY FLORY

ZONDERVAN BOOKS

Holy Disruptor
Copyright © 2025 by Amy Duggar King

Published by Zondervan, 3950 Sparks Drive SE, Suite 101, Grand Rapids, MI 49546, USA.
Zondervan is a registered trademark of The Zondervan Corporation, L.L.C., a wholly owned subsidiary of HarperCollins Christian Publishing, Inc.

Requests for information should be addressed to customercare@harpercollins.com.

Zondervan titles may be purchased in bulk for educational, business, fundraising, or sales promotional use. For information, please email SpecialMarkets@Zondervan.com.

ISBN 978-0-310-37102-1 (international trade paper edition)
ISBN 978-0-310-37001-7 (audio)

Library of Congress Cataloging-in-Publication Data

Names: Duggar King, Amy, 1986- author
Title: Holy disruptor : shattering the shiny facade by getting louder with the truth / Amy Duggar King with Susy Flory.
Description: Grand Rapids, Michigan : Zondervan Books, [2025]
Identifiers: LCCN 2025020550 (print) | LCCN 2025020551 (ebook) | ISBN 9780310369950 hardcover | ISBN 9780310369998 ebook
Subjects: LCSH: Duggar, Jim Bob—Family | Psychological abuse—Religious aspects--Christianity | Psychic trauma—Religious aspects—Christianity | Psychology, Religious
Classification: LCC BV4596.P87 D844 2025 (print) | LCC BV4596.P87 (ebook) | DDC 277.308/2092 [B]—dc23/eng/20250715
LC record available at https://lccn.loc.gov/2025020550
LC ebook record available at https://lccn.loc.gov/2025020551

Cover design: Curt Diepenhorst
Cover photography: Miles Witt Boyer
Interior design: Kristy Edwards

Printed in the United States of America

25 26 27 28 29 LBC 5 4 3 2 1

To the ones who've walked through trauma—
the kind that lingers in body, mind, and memory—
to those who were hurt by people
you were supposed to trust,
to those from complicated families
where love came with conditions
and where you were expected
to absorb the damage and never speak of it.

To the ones who've carried weight that was never yours,
to the ones who learned how to survive before
they ever learned how to rest,
to those unfairly labeled
too much, too sensitive, too different, too loud—
you were never the problem.

You are not your trauma.
You are not too broken to heal.
You are worthy of love
and of a life that feels honest, peaceful, and whole.

This book is for you.
And I pray God uses these words
to lead you there—
one truth, one step, one breakthrough at a time.

Contents

The Rules

Institute in Basic Life Principles

At the core of the IBLP system—the system my uncle Jim Bob and aunt Michelle followed religiously—is the idea that you can achieve godliness by following a specific set of rules—rules that are artificial and twisted to seem like biblical truths when in reality they are not. In this system, the rules are clearly spelled out, the consequences are severe, and utter submission is expected.

IBLP MASTER LIFE PLAN

The wife must submit to the husband and refrain from challenging him. There is a lot of talk about the importance of authority in the home, but it's as though God's idea of authority got lost in translation. Take the concept of submission. Yes, the Bible talks about wives submitting to their husbands (Ephesians 5:22), but IBLP turns that into something unrecognizable, pushing women into a corner where their voices are silenced, their needs ignored, and their existence reduced to inferior status. It's one thing to honor your husband; it's another to be treated like a robot who must follow orders without question. IBLP's interpretation completely distorts biblical marriage, creating a dynamic where men are in charge—and no one can challenge them. In fact, if a man decides his family needs to follow "the principles" (which are often his own), there's no accountability. Whatever he says goes—end of story.

But what happens when these men abuse their power? Who holds them accountable? No one. There's a huge gap in responsibility, and it's this vacuum that often leads to manipulation and abuse.

Women may not pursue independence or self-reliance. IBLP's control over women goes beyond marriage, discouraging them from seeking independence or help without their husband's permission. A wife is expected never to take matters into her own hands, financially or otherwise. Seeking counseling or guidance from anyone outside IBLP is viewed as an act of rebellion unless her husband permits it. A woman's autonomy is essentially erased, while her husband is granted absolute control.

Women must be seen and not heard—and definitely not be in charge. There are not only issues with how IBLP treats children, but also there are severe problems with how IBLP treats women. The teachings promote the idea that women are there to be *seen* but not *heard*. They're meant to be submissive to their husbands, take care of the house, and raise as many children as possible. IBLP members are raised to believe that if a woman uses birth control, she is not being totally dedicated to the Lord, which could lead to miscarriages. No form of birth control whatsoever is allowed.

Yes, children are a gift from God (Psalm 127:3), but the pressure to constantly have babies and multiply can feel more like an assembly line than a gift. Women's voices are silenced under the guise of being godly. But guess what? God gave women voices too (Proverbs 31:26)! He didn't give them a voice only to have them sit quietly in the corner while the men made all the decisions. Women are not cookie-cutter molds designed to fit one narrow purpose. We are individuals, each with our own callings and gifts. Trying to force every woman into the same box is not only harmful, but it goes against what God intended all along.

A husband has full access to his wife's body, no questions asked. Wives may not resist or be indifferent. In other words, a wife's body is her husband's property, and her needs or boundaries are considered secondary or irrelevant. This view of marriage strips away the concept of mutual respect and love, turning it into a one-sided relationship where the husband's desires take priority. This is in direct contrast to the Bible's teaching that husbands and wives should love and honor each other sacrificially (Ephesians 5:25–33). The idea of a wife as property is dehumanizing, yet IBLP clings to it as part of their definition of godly submission.

Higher education for women is strongly discouraged— "Ladies, keep it at home." The philosophy here is that a woman's primary role is to be a wife, mother, and homemaker, and anything beyond that is seen as unnecessary, even harmful. Why study to become a doctor, engineer, or even a teacher when your true calling is already mapped out for you—cleaning, cooking, and child-rearing? IBLP often pushes the idea that a woman's mind should stay focused on God's design for her, defined as serving her family. They even imply that education might corrupt her by exposing her to worldly ideas, as if knowledge itself is dangerous. The result? Many IBLP women are left feeling unprepared and limited, unable to pursue personal dreams, passions, or talents that fall outside IBLP's interpretation of biblical womanhood.

The Bible, in fact, praises wisdom and knowledge (Proverbs 1:7; 4:5–7) and even highlights women in active, valuable roles—like Deborah the judge (Judges 4–5) or Lydia the businesswoman (Acts 16:14–15).

Nothing in Scripture says women shouldn't be educated. In fact, being wise, resourceful, and knowledgeable helps them serve others better!

Women are expected to nurture a "gentle and quiet spirit," based on a narrow reading of 1 Peter 3:4. This IBLP belief implies that a woman should always be soft-spoken, gentle, and submissive, with little room for boldness or individuality. But here's the twist: While being meek and quiet on the inside, wives are simultaneously expected to strive for physical beauty to keep their husbands' attention. This creates a contradictory standard. Women are supposed to be silent and invisible in personality, yet stunning and always present. It creates constant pressure to be perfect on the outside while staying silent and compliant on the inside.

This approach contradicts Proverbs 31, which celebrates a wife's independence, business skills, and resourcefulness. God never intended for a woman's identity to be smothered by her husband's authority; instead, he created her to be a partner, not a possession. The Bible teaches that a husband should love his wife as Christ loves the church—selflessly (Ephesians 5:25). But IBLP makes it clear that a husband can be as selfish as he wants.

Women must not show bare shoulders, knees, or collarbones, for to do so is scandalous. Let's talk about modesty standards. They're intense. The Bible does encourage modesty (1 Timothy 2:9), but IBLP takes it up a thousand notches. Shoulders, collarbones, and knees are seen as so scandalous that they must always remain hidden. Think of it as the modesty Olympics—long skirts (don't even think about a slit; those must be sewn up immediately), blouses up to your neck, sleeves to cover your shoulders, and don't even dream of wearing pants if you're a female. Wearing blue jeans blurs the line of femininity, and no woman should ever want to get close to that line.

And while modesty can be beautiful, in IBLP it becomes an impossible game where individuality gets stamped out entirely.

There's no room for personal expression, no freedom to wear what feels good to you. Instead, you must blend in with other IBLP families in a sea of denim skirts and long-sleeved blouses. Being modest shouldn't mean becoming a carbon copy of everyone else, yet that's exactly what happens.

Women (and men) must not wear black clothing because it's sinful. Here's the part that will make you want to roll your eyes so hard they might get stuck. In IBLP, you're not allowed to wear black clothing—because it's "too worldly" and "too rebellious." I mean, really? Black? The color that represents mourning and humility? A color that is classy and timeless? But nope, apparently it's sinful if you wear it. You may as well be wearing a neon sign that reads "I'm a rebellious sinner" if you dare to sport anything black. This is where the absurdity of IBLP hits a new high. They take small, insignificant things—like the color of your clothes—and turn them into tests of your holiness. What the Bible actually teaches is that we're defined not by what we wear but by the love of Christ that shines through us (1 Samuel 16:7). But IBLP creates a culture where people are judged by these ridiculous standards, making them feel guilty over things that have nothing to do with salvation. It teaches that if we ever want to express ourselves in a way that doesn't perfectly align with their rules, it means we have a "heart issue," like we're all supposed to be cut from the same cloth. But that's not how God designed us to live. He created us uniquely, with different gifts, personalities, and callings—not to be silenced or squeezed into someone else's mold.

Women (and men) must avoid tattoos and piercings. Tattoos are viewed as sinful, based on Scriptures that emphasize honoring the body as God's temple. Leviticus 19:28 warns against marking the body, which IBLP interprets as maintaining purity and avoiding worldly customs. First Corinthians 6:19–20 urges believers to honor God with their bodies, and Romans 12:1–2 advises against conforming to worldly practices. Tattoos, viewed as part of secular culture, are seen as disrespectful to God's creation and a violation of biblical principles on purity and reverence.

For women in IBLP, piercing their ears is seen as a mark of bondage to the world. Apparently, it symbolizes slavery. But isn't it strange that this idea has no biblical backing? In fact, Exodus 21:6 references ear piercing as a mark of devotion. While we don't live under the Old Testament law anymore (Romans 6:14), it's funny to think that something like ear piercing, which is a simple and personal choice for many, would be twisted into a mark of disobedience. If anything, the New Testament reminds us that our freedom is found in Christ, not in outward rules or appearances (Galatians 5:1).

Women must keep their hair long—no cutting allowed. For women, it's all about the length; you need to keep it long. It's seen as a covering and a mark of femininity, and there's an emphasis on never cutting it. Now, long hair can be beautiful, sure, but it's hardly a biblical requirement. First Corinthians 11 does mention that a woman's hair is given to her for covering, but that's more about cultural respect than a hard-and-fast rule. And let's remember, we're not bound by every Old Testament or cultural standard. God doesn't judge us by the length of our hair but by the sincerity of our hearts (1 Samuel 16:7).

Children are the father's property—like goods to be owned and controlled. This mentality is woven into everything and factors into the way children are raised. The husband and father is the absolute authority, with the power to impose any rule or command, no questions asked.

IBLP's extreme standards for modesty, abstinence, and submission create a superficial "holiness" that is more about control than faith. It's a system that values obedience to man-made rules over a personal, genuine relationship with God. In Jesus' time, the Pharisees were rebuked for focusing on outward appearances while ignoring inner transformation (Matthew 23:27–28). Yet IBLP mirrors that same approach—emphasizing rules that ultimately limit rather than liberate God's people.

This ownership mentality has zero biblical basis. In fact, the Bible teaches that we are all created in God's image (Genesis 1:27). When you strip away the individuality, enforce fear-based obedience, and treat wives and children as property, you end up with a framework that promotes legalism, not love. This system doesn't cultivate true spiritual growth; it cultivates conformity and compliance. And it opens up avenues for abuse.

Children must obey out of fear (the "or else . . ." threat). One of the most manipulative aspects of IBLP is its use of fear to control behavior. Parents are told to warn their children that if they don't obey IBLP's principles, something terrible might happen to them— maybe a car accident, a disease, or other punishments from God. This fear-based approach is not only harmful but directly contradicts the message of grace and freedom we find in the Bible. Scripture says that God's kindness leads us to repentance (Romans 2:4), not fear of punishment. Yet IBLP twists this truth, making God out to be a harsh judge waiting to smite anyone who steps out of line. It's spiritual manipulation, plain and simple.

In what seems to be an odd paradox, children are left unsupervised to figure things out on their own. IBLP teaches that God will watch over and protect children, and yet I've witnessed firsthand how this belief can lead to neglectful practices. There is a surprising lack of hands-on parenting. I've seen toddlers wandering alone in wide-open fields, almost like cattle. There seems to be the mindset that Jesus will protect their children, so there's little emphasis on being watchful or present as a parent. I've seen kids in IBLP environments jump on car hoods like monkeys, wander acres away without anyone noticing, and even get dangerously close to sticking their little hands into the blades of an air conditioner. There's poison ivy and snakes—so many risks—and yet the kids are just left to roam free.

While it's great to let children explore and have adventures, there has to be a balance. You still have to protect them. But from what I've seen, the belief that Jesus will watch over them leads to parents failing to guard and defend them. It's not just a laid-back parenting style; it's a hands-off approach that overlooks basic safety.

Another serious concern has to do with what happens when a child has experienced abuse or trauma that has never been addressed or healed. The pain doesn't just disappear; it often gets acted out, sometimes upon other innocent children. There is a real danger in letting kids run wild without guidance or supervision. When no one is watching, they are denied protection—not just from wild animals but from kids who may be carrying deep, unhealed wounds of their own. And that kind of harm is just as real, if not more so.

Children must instantly obey and are not allowed to think for themselves. One of the most troubling rules IBLP teaches is the emphasis on instant obedience. Children should be programmed to obey. This concept teaches that children must obey their parents immediately—no questions, no delays, no thought. Just do it the second you're told. It's not just about obedience; it's about control.

That's all well and good, right? Except for the fact that this doesn't give children any space to think for themselves, process their emotions, or even question their parents' decisions. If you can't think for yourself, how can you truly learn to obey wisely? This isn't the way God designed children to learn, especially when it comes to issues like discipline and respect. God doesn't want us to be robots who simply carry out orders. He wants us to understand right from wrong, grow in wisdom, and develop a personal relationship with him. Instant obedience doesn't allow any of that. Yet every one of my nineteen cousins were pros at it.

Children are to follow the programmed life—homeschooled, isolated, and uninformed. Kids, don't even think about having worldly interactions. IBLP encourages strict homeschooling, and while that type of education in itself isn't bad, the problem is that the curriculum is created by IBLP and is designed to program a child, not educate them. The curriculum is severely limited and lacks any real education on body safety, boundaries, or understanding what abuse or sexual assault is. In IBLP's view, teaching children about these topics could corrupt them, so they're left completely unprepared. This lack of information creates a dangerous vulnerability, as children have no tools to recognize abuse or speak out if something wrong happens. The Bible encourages protecting the innocent (Matthew 18:6), but this curriculum leaves children unaware and unprotected.

The IBLP system isolates kids from real-world experiences and teaches them to reject outside perspectives. If you question anything, you're either seen as a troublemaker or you're just "not getting it." Children are raised in this bubble, completely unaware of the world around them. They grow up thinking that anything outside of the IBLP-approved world is dangerous and sinful. And when they finally step out into the world, they're powerless to live with confidence in today's society.

Children must undergo physical discipline—in a misinterpretation of "spare the rod, spoil the child." IBLP teaches that physical discipline isn't just allowed; it's encouraged. Corporal punishment, often with a rod, is seen as the best way to ensure "instant obedience" and mold children into compliant, submissive adults. The Bible does mention discipline (Proverbs 13:24), but IBLP's interpretation of it is harsh and unwavering. They treat physical punishment as a godly method to bend a child to the parents' will, often without regard for the child's mental or emotional well-being. This approach not only breaks a child's spirit but also damages the parent-child bond, replacing trust with fear. Discipline should be about teaching and guiding, not instilling terror. You can parent successfully in a way that never involves physical harm.

Children learn obedience best through blanket training— punishment by physical force. One of the most heartbreaking parts of IBLP's teaching is something called blanket training. Now, this isn't just about training a child to sit on a blanket (as some may think); it's about using physical force to control a baby or toddler. Parents place their child on a blanket, and whenever the child tries to move off it, they're spanked. The idea is that the child must learn obedience by being punished for their natural behavior—like, you know, crawling away.

This is messed up on so many levels. First, it teaches children to fear their parents, not love and trust them. Second, it breaks the child's ability to trust their own instincts, creating confusion and emotional damage. It's abuse. And yet, because it's wrapped in the guise of "training," IBLP insists that it's the right way to raise children. But anyone who has ever worked with children or understands child development knows this approach doesn't foster obedience, but rather breaks their spirit and creates deep emotional scars. And let's not forget the parents who think they're doing the right thing but are in reality following a script that doesn't line up with biblical love.

Daughters are expected to have their courtship overseen by both sets of parents in "godly" matchmaking. Daughters are discouraged from dreaming about falling in love or meeting someone organically. In this world, the idea of love is replaced with duty, and marriage becomes a family-arranged transaction rather than a genuine partnership built on mutual affection.

A typical IBLP courtship involves no hand-holding, no private conversations, and absolutely no flirting. After all, flirting is seen as ungodly, as though showing a hint of attraction to someone is akin to moral failure. Even smiling too long at someone or winking could be seen as a red flag. Courting couples are kept under the watchful eyes of parents or an appointed chaperone, and any sign of genuine chemistry or emotional connection gets quashed as temptation.

By stripping courtship of romance, IBLP ensures that young people go into marriage with minimal emotional intimacy, which can lead to a marriage that feels more like a partnership in a business arrangement than a loving bond. But doesn't the Bible say love is a gift (1 Corinthians 13:13)? Somehow, the romantic parts of the Bible are entirely skipped over in IBLP.

It's all very proper and, well, stifling. Where's the chance for these young people to actually get to *know* each other? It's ironic, too, because IBLP emphasizes self-control, yet they never let their young people practice it. How can you build self-control when you're always shielded from situations that would actually help you develop it? This approach breeds obedience and submission, leaving no room for choice. In the end, the daughter's dad transfers his authority to the new husband under what is called the umbrella of authority. As long as the wife has protection from her spouse or father, she will thrive in life.

Interracial relationships are seriously frowned upon. One of the most painful teachings in IBLP is the discouragement—sometimes outright ban—on interracial relationships. People are told to stay with their own kind. But God makes it clear that he looks at the heart, not at skin color (1 Samuel 16:7). Jesus showed us how to cross cultural and social boundaries to share God's love with everyone. Think of the Samaritan woman at the well (John 4), a powerful story of Jesus breaking down racial and cultural barriers. Galatians 3:28 reminds us that, in Christ, "there is neither Jew nor Gentile, neither slave nor free, nor is there male and female, for you are all one in Christ Jesus." There's simply no biblical basis for restricting relationships by race. God's kingdom is diverse, filled with people from every tribe, language, and nation (Revelation 7:9). So where is the love in saying that people can't be together because of the color of their skin? It's about as un-Christlike as you can get.

If there is ever a need for counseling, it must be provided by an IBLP elder member. Professional counselors are considered unsafe and could ruin a person's potential to serve the Lord such that their relationship with him can never be the same. All outside counseling, especially anything resembling therapy from licensed professionals, isn't just discouraged; it's deemed dangerous and disobedient. The IBLP system teaches that the "worldly" wisdom of psychologists or trauma specialists is rooted in rebellion against God.

In IBLP, counseling becomes a form of correction that points at faults and acknowledges pain. People are told to search their hearts for hidden sin. *What did I do to make a man or my brother stumble?* To be as godly as possible, they must submit more and forgive faster. So victims must smile, offer mercy, and pardon the sin. Yes, the Bible tells us to forgive seventy times seven, but forgiveness doesn't eliminate justice. Incest isn't just a sin; it's a criminal act. Unfortunately, many sufferers within IBLP keep living with abusers in the same household.

In this environment, image is everything. The goal isn't really about healing, but rather about silence. *Keep the family intact. Avoid shame. Don't let the truth spread beyond the walls of home, church, or family camp.* Who knows, however, what kind of counseling advice will be given if the person being counseled isn't reporting emotional or physical abuse?

WHEN THE SPOTLIGHT HIDES THE CRACKS

My cousins had so many rules to follow, and those rules were strictly enforced. Physical punishment happened for infractions, but it all took place behind closed doors. I never saw anyone get spanked, although my uncle spanked me once when I was a little girl during an innocent game of hide-and-seek for telling a white lie about my hiding place. (In my defense, it was a *game*.)

My aunt carried a big stick or rod in the car with her children. It sat up on the dashboard, and the name of the stick was *Encouragement*. There were at least half a dozen rubber rods around the house kept on display and ready for use by my aunt and uncle. They never spanked my cousins in front of me, but I saw the kids' eyes widen when Aunt Michelle said, head tilted, in her quiet, sweet voice, "Do we need some encouragement?"

The Duggars went on to become role models for millions of families—girls, boys, men, and women. They were showcased as the gold standard of Christian living, praised for their faith, honored for their family structure, and admired as the ideal example of godliness. They weren't just a well-known family; they provided the blueprint for how others were told to live, worship, and raise their children.

Yet they knew about the horrifying events that had taken place before the television show *19 Kids and Counting* ever got started. And the show was filmed anyway. The network was left completely in the dark.

IBLP taught everyone to closely follow the rules and to fear the consequences. My aunt and uncle preached godliness and modeled it on television for the world to see. But behind the scenes, certain issues were never dealt with. Instead of facing situations honestly, they hid, minimized, or ignored some things. As a result, people were hurt, some very deeply. The refusal to confront the truth didn't just impact my family; it left many others carrying the weight of that silence. And the fallout is still being felt.

Introduction

Getting Louder

For years, my story has been told for me. I'm *that* Amy— "Crazy Cousin Amy"—the happy, spunky niece of one of the most famous families in America, the Duggars.

For ten seasons and 109 episodes as a featured member of the smash-hit cable television show *19 Kids and Counting*, I felt like I had no control over how I was presented to the public. My uncle Jim Bob Duggar wouldn't listen to me, and the network took orders directly from him. I wanted to scream from the rooftops, "I'm not crazy or wild!"

Imagine a world where normal activities like wearing a bathing suit or going to the movies is considered a sin. This is what the patriarch of my family, my uncle, called "ungodly behavior." Wearing anything bright yellow or black is wrong. No one goes to college. Kissing is absolutely forbidden. Wearing shorts, even on the hottest days? Forget it.

I've never done drugs in my life, don't like to party, and don't have a police record, but because I was different from all my cousins, I was considered the black sheep. I wasn't allowed to be myself and had to hide who I was if I had any hope of being accepted in my aunt and uncle's home. I loved going to the mall with my friends, having full-blown concerts in my car, going to dances, and being adventurous, but at Uncle Jim Bob's home, I was made to feel ashamed for being who I was—a normal teenage girl.

Not only was I singled out and shamed, but I was lied to as well. I'm still trying to untangle the lies—some of them televised across the country and even the world—from the truth.

Now it's finally time to tell my own story.

It's not all black-and-white. My childhood was fun in a lot of ways, and I spent almost every single day with my cousins, from my oldest cousin Josh pushing us girls in the Radio Flyer wagon down a huge hill as we laughed and screamed with joy to being surrounded by television crews under bright lights and traveling the world together. Doors were flung open to us because of the Duggar name.

I have been told stories about my family by many different people, including my mom, family friends, and people in my community. My own memories are twisted and tangled threads of good and bad, fun and fear, order and chaos, love and pain, truth and lies, godliness and evil. There were painful, complicated moments where I felt uninvited, rejected, and too much or not enough, as well as moments that were loving, good, warm, and comforting.

In a way, I miss the closeness of our Duggar family, but I do not miss the legalism or the judgment.

This is the story of a little girl born into what would become a very famous family, but who had a deep heartache and trauma of her own that no one outside her house knew much about. My uncle and aunt seemed to have the perfect family; mine was anything but.

This is also a story of escaping control, manipulation, and abuse from almost everyone close to me as I fought to find out who I truly was. Getting to know myself and finding my voice took some time, but I finally discovered it, and I am no longer afraid to stand up for what is right. What I experienced through the years with my uncle and aunt and their nineteen kids, along with my own grandparents and parents, has helped me grow into a truth seeker, a truth teller, and a holy disruptor.

My faith has been my anchor, guiding me through even the hardest moments. But that doesn't mean this journey has been easy. In fact, it's been deeply painful—because I've seen and experienced things that I know must grieve the heart of God. Watching people twist faith for their own gain, witnessing deception where there should have been truth, and feeling the weight of betrayal from those who claim to love God—it's heartbreaking. Yet through it all, I've held on to the certainty that God sees, knows, and cares. Even when my heart aches, I find comfort in knowing that his love remains constant.

As I navigate the wild seas of my life, the beautiful story of Jesus calming the wind and the rough waters resonates deep within me, offering a powerful symbol of the peace he desires for every corner of our lives (Mark 4:35–41). Being a holy disruptor is all about standing up for the truth in order to break the trauma and toxic cycles in a family. It's about saying, "This has gone on long enough and it stops with me!" Though it can be costly to be a holy disruptor, I have learned to be filled with an inner calm that comes only from knowing Jesus. As I continue to face the wind and waves, I am at peace, and I willingly stand against anything or anyone who breaks the heart of God.

As you read on, you'll see that I'm not hiding anything under the rug—in fact, the rug has been completely pulled away. Settle in for a story that reveals a world of unrealistic expectations and manipulation—a world where I had to untangle a web of carefully crafted lies while fighting to protect my own mental health. It's a journey of breaking free from toxic cycles, confronting painful truths, and finding the faith to keep going. Consider this my unfiltered testimony.

And if your story is anything like mine, I want you to hear this loud and clear: No matter what chaos or trauma you're experiencing, if you're willing to become a holy disruptor, sweet freedom is waiting to embrace you on the other side.

I was always told, "You are too loud, Amy." Well, folks, if you ask me, I haven't been loud enough. And I'm about to get even louder.

CHAPTER
ONE

How It All Started

19 Kids and Counting[1] first aired on TLC on September 29, 2008, following the daily life of my uncle Jim Bob Duggar and my aunt Michelle, along with their large and growing family. The Duggars became massively popular for their unconventional lifestyle that emphasized extremely conservative Christian values, homeschooling, and the challenges and rewards of raising a large family.

An intact family with nineteen well-behaved biological children who often dressed alike felt rare and fascinating to many viewers. The show highlighted close-knit family dynamics with a focus on the children's roles in helping care for one another and the household. Strict adherence to religious beliefs, including the practice of courtship rather than dating and strict modesty, also attracted a large viewership and sparked curiosity. They were also well-known for their hair! No matter what kind of weather we were having, not a strand of Uncle Jim Bob's or Aunt Michelle's hair was ever out of place. My aunt's hair

---

1. When the reality show launched on TLC in 2008, the original title was *17 Kids and Counting*. This title quickly changed to *18 Kids and Counting*, and finally *19 Kids and Counting*. To simplify, I'll use the final version of the title.

was iconic, with big curls that bounced perfectly—courtesy of cases of Aqua Net hair spray. The Duggars' wholesome image and the continuous arrival of new babies kept audiences tuned in, making the original show and its spin-offs some of the network's most popular programs.

But though everyone seemed to know who America's Favorite Family was, they were just my family. Their house became a sanctuary for me from my own chaotic home. I loved how everything felt well-ordered, with my aunt's quiet, warm voice directing traffic while quiet classical music filled the air. My cousins would be doing homework or taking care of younger siblings. There was a lot of laughter in the house and a lot of work too. My grandma, who lived with my uncle and aunt, did all the laundry—seventy loads a week—folding it and putting it away in one huge family closet. For meals every day, there was an assembly line, like at a buffet restaurant, and the older kids helped the younger ones fill their plates. Between meals, we played games for hours on the long dinner table.

At twenty-one years old, I was a hardworking nanny, caring for the children of some of the city's affluent families who knew they could trust me to protect their kids and invite a lot of fun into their homes. I had great references and kept busy with work, but I always made time for my cousins; the younger ones were so full of life. Sometimes I'd spend the whole day over there if they weren't filming.

When *19 Kids and Counting* first aired, I kept my distance and never really got involved in what was going on. But that didn't last long. One random Tuesday morning in 2008, I took off from work to drive to my cousins' house to pick up my grandma for an appointment. I drove down the road toward my aunt and uncle's house, my windows rolled down and my '90s rock music blaring, without a care in the world. But as I approached their driveway, I turned the volume down to a whisper, knowing they wouldn't appreciate my "sinful" music. I punched in the code to the automatic gate and drove up the driveway, taking in the fleet of open trailers full of camera equipment. The show was still new but already consistently drawing a large audience of dedicated viewers for the network.

Dang, I don't want to deal with this today, I thought. So I parked the car and called my grandma. "Hey, they're filming," I said. "I don't want to walk in on them. Can you just meet me outside?"

Filming the show had become the family's thing, a passion that already consumed much of their time and energy. From the very beginning, I had no desire to be part of it and never asked to join in. The constant presence of cameras, along with the spotlight, wasn't what I was searching for. I preferred my privacy and my unrecorded life, happy to be a normal, ordinary person. I'm a homebody at heart who values relationships and enjoys the simple things in life. I wasn't looking for any extra attention. But my grandma, the ever-persistent meddler, had a different idea. "Sweetiebabe, I have a few things I need to get done," she replied. "It might take a few minutes. Can you help me in my room? Please just come inside."

I could tell she had an agenda, and once she set her mind on something, there was no changing it. I adored her, but I also knew it was Grandma's way or the highway—with everything. She always chose where we ate, sticking to the places she liked, and if she had a particular idea for an outing, that's exactly what we were going to do. So when she told me to come inside my cousins' house, I knew there was no point in saying no. She'd sit there all day, tapping her foot, until I walked through that door!

Okay, Mema. Reluctantly I got out of the car and walked up to the house. Slowly I turned the doorknob and went in, walking through the large house as quietly as I could. But to get to my grandma's room, I had to make it past my cousins and their parents, who were in the living area fully assembled on the L-shaped sofa, hands folded in "choir position," with cameras rolling. Everyone, including my aunt Michelle, listened intently as Uncle Jim Bob announced they were going to pick a chaperone for their oldest brother, Josh, because Josh and Anna were the new couple who had recently started courting.

I loved my oldest cousin, who was just a year younger than me. I had grown up with Josh because my mother, Deanna, is Jim Bob's only sibling, and our families were close. But right now, I wasn't the least bit interested in being pulled into this chaperone-selection process. I just wanted to get to Grandma's room and get out of that part of the house.

I remained quiet, carefully making my way around the edges of the room as I aimed for my grandma's door, which was connected to the living room and accessed through the large laundry room leading to her side of the house. I waved to all my cousins while trying to be as silent as possible. As I tiptoed along, my uncle started drawing names from a hat. All the kids were so excited; they all wanted to be the chosen chaperone for Josh and Anna, mainly because it meant going somewhere fun and getting out of the house.

I couldn't help myself. I laughed out loud just a little! I mean, how could I not? The idea that this engaged couple needed someone with them to ensure they didn't show any physical affection was absurd to me. To the Duggar family, kissing was the ultimate sin. Being flirty, or touching of any kind, wasn't allowed, except for an occasional awkward side hug. They weren't allowed to fog up any windows, if you know what I mean.

One of the producers, Sean, heard my little chuckle and looked over at me. "Who are you?"

I stopped. "Oh, I'm just their cousin, Amy. I'm here to pick up Grandma. I'm so sorry if I'm interrupting your shot. I'm just trying to get to her room."

"Would you like to be the chaperone for Josh and Anna?" he said.

I laughed again and said, "No offense to their beliefs, but I'd ditch my chaperone duties. I'd let them do pretty much whatever they wanted. I mean, after all, they are considered adults."

The producer's eyes widened, and he smiled, saying, "You are going to be TV gold. Why don't you hop into the mix?"

What! Heck no was my first reaction. *I love my cousins, but I'm different. I have my own life.* Also, I didn't fully grasp what Sean meant or what being recruited onto the show would mean for me. I knew people watched the show, but I truly didn't understand how popular it was. I had no idea there were already millions and millions of viewers. But I loved my cousins and wanted to continue to be part of their lives, even if that meant being on TV.

In a daze, I made my way to Grandma's door. "Uh, plans have changed," I said. Grandma seemed more than happy to reschedule her appointment.

And that's how I joined the show—all because of a quiet chuckle. And slowly, over time, I became a featured character, front and center.

After that first episode, I was invited to film episodes with my uncle, aunt, and cousins the entire week. I loved it because each week brought a new adventure. I loved being spontaneous. I never knew what I would be doing next, and the schedule could change at a moment's notice. I didn't have a set filming schedule. I just knew that Tuesdays and Thursdays were devoted to whatever they needed me for, so I began to take those filming days off from my job.

At first, I felt strange, with huge cameras looming all around me, a boom microphone at the end of a long metal arm hovering above my head, and a microphone wire tucked underneath my shirt with a battery pack shoved into my back pocket. The mic itself was taped to the inside of my top. I was instructed by the producer not to look at the cameras—to pretend they weren't there and to not draw attention to myself in any way. To my surprise, ignoring the cameras came naturally to me, partly because the film crew was down to earth and hilarious, and they made me feel at ease in this strange new world. I felt welcomed and I loved them all!

But let's be honest, if you watched the show, you know I stuck out like a sore thumb. My medium-length hair (not long and cascading like my cousins'), distressed jeans (gasp!), and a graphic T-shirt proved that I didn't quite fit in with the squeaky-clean image my other family members portrayed.

Ratings spiked whenever I was on the show, so my camera time began to grow. My bouncy personality also quickly earned me a memorable nickname: "Crazy Cousin Amy."

At first, I pushed back. "Can I just be Cousin Amy?" I asked my uncle Jim Bob. "Why does the word *crazy* have to be in my title? Would you like the word *crazy* to be associated with *your* name?"

"Oh, Amy, we're just adding in a little fun. Don't worry about it," he said with a laugh, dismissing my concerns.

But after the first episode, I knew the nickname was going to stick. I hate to break it to you, but the crazy cousin Amy you knew from television was just the character they made me out to be. It is not the real me. Sure, I can be bubbly and my personality is breezy and carefree, but there's so much more to me beneath the surface. I have a moral compass that guides me; I am strong in my faith; and I'm not a wild soul meandering aimlessly through life. I didn't know how to stand up for myself back then, and I had never really learned how to fight for what I needed or protect my boundaries, so I often found myself shrinking when in difficult situations.

What *was* real is still real today: I enjoy making people laugh and spreading joy to those around me. I am a person of depth and substance and a seeker of truth, even the hard truths. That is the Amy I wish I could've shown to the world. Even so, I'm proud of the journey that brought me to this place of self-awareness and strength.

During filming days, I was already so emotionally drained and worn down from everything I was going through in my own personal, private, untelevised life that I just didn't have the strength left to face another problem. You'll find out more about why in the coming chapters, but for now, let's just say that my parents were in a deeply unhappy relationship. And I was trying hard to portray a shiny, happy facade. My smiles and bubbly personality masked my sadness, and my role in the TV series became a coping mechanism. Many times, I felt like I was barely holding it together, and any additional challenge seemed overwhelming. I truly felt like just one more thing could completely break me. I was stuck in survival mode, and even though I wanted to fight back, I simply didn't have the energy.

Everything is different now. I am no longer in survival mode. I am healing and ready to share the real me with the world. My goal is to live a life true to myself, one that reflects my values and beliefs, and to offer a sincere, heartfelt apology for not doing so sooner.

Living in truth, despite the challenges it brings, is always worth it. It's worth facing misunderstandings, criticism, and uncomfortable conversations. At the heart of it all, embracing authenticity means living freely, which is a priceless freedom.

All my life I was taught to stay quiet, to keep my feelings to myself, and to just go along with what others wanted. As a young child I felt invisible, like no one was listening to me or cared about what I was going through. It was as though my emotions didn't matter and my voice wasn't worth hearing.

As I got older, I fell into the harmful pattern of letting others define who I was. Growing up without a healthy example of love or respect in a relationship, I didn't know what it truly meant to be treated with kindness and dignity. This lack of understanding set me up for failure when it came to dating. I found myself in relationships with men who cheated, belittled me, or had anger issues. Deep down, I thought this was all I deserved because my self-worth was so low. I didn't believe

I was worthy of anything better, so I stayed in toxic situations far too long, tolerating behavior that I now see as unacceptable.

Along the way, I became a people pleaser, constantly bending over backward to make others happy, even if it meant sacrificing my own well-being. It wasn't until I found my voice that I began to realize how much I had been settling. It was a painful, yet necessary, lesson in learning how I truly deserved to be treated.

When I became part of one of the most widely known reality TV shows in America, I found myself trapped once again, but this time by the media. The outside world, with all its judgments and assumptions, began to dictate my narrative. Instead of owning my story, I let the media shape it for me.

For years, I wrestled with where I fit into my family, why I felt so different, and what my true purpose was. There were times when I wondered whether I would ever feel like I belonged. During one of the lowest points of my life, I had a conversation with a close friend and mentor. She didn't know it then, but what she said after I poured my heart out to her would change the course of my life. Depleted and desperate to understand why I always felt like I wasn't doing enough, saying enough, or being enough for anyone in my life, I told her I felt like one big disappointment. "I don't understand my life," I told her, feeling utterly lost.

Without missing a beat, she looked right at me and with remarkable compassion said something I'll never forget. "Amy, you're not afraid to question what you've been taught. You're bold. You confront evil head-on. Don't ever let anyone tell you otherwise. You are doing God's work."

She said those words with such conviction that I began to realize my willingness to question and stand up for truth might not be a flaw but a strength—an essential part of who God created me to be. For so long, I had struggled with the pressure to conform to what was expected of me, especially when it came to my family and faith. I had questioned everything, yet I doubted whether my questioning was okay or if it made me less of a believer.

"You are not a mistake," she continued on, looking straight into my eyes and my soul. "*You* are a holy disruptor."

In that moment her words reminded me of something crucial: God doesn't make mistakes. He created me with purpose, with the courage to ask hard questions. That conversation was a turning point for me because I realized being a holy disruptor doesn't mean rejecting God or his truth. Being a holy disruptor means standing up against practices and beliefs that are harmful, even when they are presented as being in accordance with the character of Jesus.

It's about recognizing when the traditions and rules of your own upbringing don't honor God or promote true love and peace and then having the courage to speak out. It means challenging authority that seeks to control instead of uplift and making a conscious decision to live differently. A holy disruptor is someone who sees things as they are, calls out what's wrong, and commits to personal growth and well-being. It's about acknowledging the harsh realities of the world and taking a stand against its injustices, even when it's uncomfortable or unpopular.

When I was a little girl, I put my family on a pedestal. As I became a teenager, I didn't think for a second that there were any secrets or hidden struggles in our family. Growing up, I believed the image my Duggar family portrayed to the world was the truth.

A holy disruptor is someone who sees things as they are, calls out what's wrong, and commits to personal growth and well-being. It's about acknowledging the harsh realities of the world and taking a stand against its injustices.

I was living in a bubble, but I never questioned it. I assumed everything was as it appeared and took what my uncle told me at face value. I thought perfection existed, and I believed that's exactly what the Duggar family represented—the ideal family with no flaws or issues, just perfect harmony. I had bought into that image completely because I wanted that dream to become my reality someday.

But then one day everything came crashing down. While the Duggar house seemed perfectly run and my cousins perfectly behaved, a very dark cloud was hovering just out of sight. All was not as perfect as it seemed on the television screen.

Have you ever seen the Jim Carrey movie *The Truman Show*? For most of the film, Truman thinks his manufactured, televised life is normal and everything is happy-go-lucky—until the day he literally hits the wall of his artificial universe and realizes that his entire existence has been a lie. A very public lie.

I hit the wall too, and only then did I truly realize I wasn't meant to blend in or stay quiet. I was made to disrupt, to question, and to lead others toward a better, more honest way of living. Discarding the old Crazy Cousin Amy persona and embracing the role of a holy disruptor has taught me that I have value, my voice matters, and my boldness is a gift. Because I wasn't meek and mild, my ability to be different protected me from a lot of evils, including being sexually abused.

I am beginning to see myself through a lens of resilience and grace, especially in moments when it feels difficult to go against the grain and stand up for what I think is right.

What have I had to stand up against? You're about to find out. I'm here to tell the truth about what I have been through, to push myself to my limits, and to force myself to confront parts of myself and my past that I would prefer to leave buried.

This is me. The true me. The funny, confident character who viewers saw on the show was actually a frightened girl who felt manipulated and powerless. I often found myself going along with whatever the producers told me to do or hinted that I should do because it would make good TV. The show was such a whirlwind that I never stopped to consider what I truly wanted or how I was being portrayed.

For those of you who were annoyed with me or even hated my character on the show, I get it! I'm not here to change your mind. The damage has already been done. Instead, I'm here to offer an apology.

I'm sorry I didn't speak up for myself when I should have.

I'm sorry I felt so weak.

I'm sorry I wasn't true to who I really am.

Here's the truth: The real Amy Duggar, the woman God created me to be, is not someone who stays silent. I'm not someone who just goes with the flow or lets things slide in order to protect wrongdoings—at least not anymore. I've learned that my voice matters. And I've realized that staying quiet doesn't help anyone, least of all myself.

I know who I am today. I'm a holy disruptor, and you will see in the following pages that I won't be quiet anymore. I will no longer conform to systems and patterns that distort God's truth—even when family is involved. It's the only way to truly live in peace.

CHAPTER
TWO

Back When Fun Was Free

I didn't live far from my aunt and uncle's house on Osage Street in Springdale, Arkansas. A valley separated our homes, with huge oak trees lining a beautiful walking path. When Uncle Jim Bob and Aunt Michelle's firstborn son, Josh, was four, he started walking the dirt path between our properties to play with me. I called him Joshy. My aunt would watch him until she couldn't see him anymore, and then she'd call our home phone so Grandma Duggar could watch him the rest of the way. We were so close and loved playing together each day until the sun went down.

I loved my hometown. It was the kind of place where downtown festivals brought everyone together, and a trip to the grocery store meant running into people you knew. Growing up in Springdale in the 1990s meant growing up in the Ozarks—family farms, cattle pastures, and winding country roads surrounded by rolling green hills. It had the charm of a small-town community, even as big corporations like Tyson, J.B. Hunt, and Walmart shaped its growth.

In our valley, the muddy patches of dirt were our playground, where Josh and I would craft the finest mud pies, complete with acorn toppings for decoration. We could watch the train come through a huge field. We were always playing tag, setting up stores and using rocks for money, and marking everything up with sidewalk chalk. In the kitchen, we loved mixing up weird ingredients like ranch, mustard, and grape jelly. I loved going with Grandma to her real estate showings, and sometimes Josh would come along too. On sunny days we'd race each other down the dirt path, playing chase until we were out of breath.

It was pure fun, just kids being kids and loving life, staying outside until dinnertime. Josh always made me laugh, and we got along great. Our bond was strong, and we loved to tease each other. When we began filming the show, every time I would leave their house, I'd say teasingly, "I love everybody except for Josh." We'd all laugh.

I started school a year before Josh, and even then we were inseparable. He was homeschooled, so I could still see him almost every day. As I got older, Josh's family began to grow, and it felt like my uncle and aunt were always announcing another pregnancy. Having a new cousin was always exciting, especially because I was an only child, but it sure seemed to happen really often. As the years went by, I had a never-ending supply of cousins, and I adored them all! Life got even better when my cousins moved to a home on a big plot of land right across from my school.

I attended a Christian private school, where most of the students came from picture-perfect families with beautiful homes, white picket fences, and even the occasional basement bowling alley. Some of my classmates' families even had private jets. I grew up modestly, with very few extras. We didn't have a lot of money for vacations or special outings, but I was grateful for the trips we got to take to the zoo or an amusement park. My grandma paid for my schooling, making great sacrifices to send me to such a prestigious place. She wanted to ensure I had a strong biblical foundation for life.

Despite the stark differences between my life and that of my classmates, I didn't have time to compare myself to other kids; I worried instead about when the next brawl between my parents would happen, when the next explosive argument would end with my dad throwing something. My homelife was unhealthy and unstable, and I didn't have the bandwidth to think about comparing myself to others. It was hard to sleep well or study for school and I had trouble paying attention in class because of how intense the tension was at home.

While we didn't take luxury vacations, Joshy and I had our own share of adventures. We went to Six Flags in Arlington, Texas, or Silver Dollar City in Branson, Missouri, and I love all the memories we made. I'll never forget the time our family RV broke down near an old campsite. Instead of heading to our planned destination in Texas, we decided to stay and spend a week there. The place had a rusty old waterslide that looked like it might fall apart at any moment and a river that was perfect for canoeing. I've always loved the outdoors, and I vividly remember sitting in the middle of the canoe while Grandma and Grandpa Duggar struggled to work together paddling, eventually landing us in a swampy area where a water moccasin tried to slither in alongside us.

Looking back, those years with my young cousins, my grandma, and the rest of my family were the foundation of my childhood—at least the parts I *want* to remember. The truth is, I compartmentalized the good and the bad. Later on there was plenty of bad. But the good times were filled with love, adventure, and a closeness that made even the simplest days feel extraordinary. We didn't watch TV or spend hours glued to other kinds of screens. Instead, we climbed trees, picked apples, played in the dirt, and spent entire days outside. As a young girl, those simple moments taught me that real joy isn't found in material things; it's found in the time we spend with the people who matter most. My grandma was so wise, always weaving life lessons into everyday moments, reminding me that the best things in life aren't things at all.

My school was right across the field from my cousins' place, so during recess, my cousins would line up and wave at me from across the way. If I was feeling particularly adventurous and wanted to escape for a little while, I'd squeeze my way through the barbed-wire fence and make my way across the pasture while carefully avoiding the cow patties. With all the land my aunt and uncle owned plus an hour-long recess, I could go on a little adventure to see my cousins almost every single school day.

I loved being an only child. I liked my alone time and enjoyed the quiet. But I also loved being at my cousins' house. It always felt like a never-ending party. We made rock soup, and when it rained, we played in the mud. We'd spend hours outside playing hide-and-seek, carving sticks, and playing games like freeze tag. We stayed outside until we heard Aunt Michelle's whistle—a God-given talent for a small person like my aunt. It's honestly the loudest whistle I've ever heard, and it got the attention of all of us, even when we were acres away. As soon as we heard it, we'd all race toward the back door, laughing.

Everywhere inside and outside, kids were laughing, playing chess, singing, practicing the piano, and being creative with huge cardboard boxes. We didn't need much to have fun—just one another's company, our imaginations, and the freedom to explore. Those experiences were filled with so much joy and remain some of the most cherished memories of my childhood.

My aunt and uncle's house always smelled of warm, fluffy yeast rolls coming out of the oven. The pantry was like a small grocery store, and my cousins were allowed to eat whatever they liked. We usually chose slices of cheese and uncooked ramen noodles. Aunt Michelle rarely bought potato chips, so ramen noodles were crunchy, just like chips. We all loved them. My cousins also loved to eat pickles any chance they got, plus cold canned vegetables and ravioli right out of the can. The commercial-grade freezer was stocked with hundreds of microwavable burritos, and the enormous fridge contained endless gallons of sweet tea. Everything was meticulously organized, and the home's one big family closet was coded by size and a rainbow of colors.

All of my cousins got along, with no arguments or bad attitudes. The boys didn't tease the girls, and everyone had good days—every single day. Uncle Jim Bob seemed happy to provide for his growing family, and he always hugged and kissed my aunt, which made their home feel loving and safe. I admired my aunt and uncle's marriage— the way they truly cared for each other, the little gestures of kindness, the unspoken understanding between them. It was the kind of love that felt calm and steady, something I seldom saw in my own home but longed to experience for myself.

Before the camera crews arrived, and along with it the worldwide popularity, my uncle's family had its own ways of doing things and were heavily influenced by Institute in Basic Life Principles (IBLP), a nondenominational, fundamentalist Christian organization that teaches how to succeed in life by following strict principles identified and taught by the founder, an American minister named Bill Gothard. IBLP offers seminars for ministry, participates in community outreach, mentors troubled youth, and has an international ministry, along with providing a homeschool curriculum for families like the Duggars, who hope to develop character in their children.

My cousins all had chores, which they called "jurisdictions," with wall charts to keep everyone highly organized and on task—from breaks and schooling to free time and lunch. Schedules were a big part of their lives and meticulously planned out down to the minute. The particular rules of the Duggar household were laminated, together with principles from IBLP, adorning the walls with definitions of the desired virtues and values:

- **Design:** How and Why God Made Me
- **Authority:** Our Response to God-Ordained Leadership
- **Responsibility:** Cleansing the Conscience
- **Suffering:** Surrendering to the Hurts Inflicted upon Me
- **Ownership:** Properly Handling Material Possessions
- **Freedom:** Escaping the Bondage of Moral Impurity
- **Success:** How to Fulfill Our God-Given Purpose

Traditional success in the eyes of the world was considered to be "of the devil," such as fancy cars; gaudy, oversize jewelry; mansions; and designer clothes. Appearance mattered greatly, however. My boy cousins were allowed to wear only jeans and collared shirts; their hair always had to be cut short and neatly gelled. My girl cousins wore long dresses with big pilgrim-like collars. Underneath their skirts were pantaloons—something you'd see in the Victorian era—big, white, cottony balloon or capri pants that were tapered at the ankle in order to remain extra-modest. None of them had a say in how they presented themselves. The girls couldn't cut their hair or even get a trim for the longest time, and after years of begging their dad, he finally let them layer their hair when they were teens, with the option to perm or highlight it if they wanted to. I bought the girls their first hair straightener, but the Duggar rule remained: Your hair is your glory, and it was considered more feminine and godlier to have long locks.

The whole family wore matching or color-coordinated outfits on every outing. I remember when one of the boys began to show a glimmer of fashion sense with his clothes, wearing bright colors and bow ties. My uncle explained to him that the colors he was choosing to wear, although fun, were not masculine. I wasn't in the room when this conversation took place, but I can certainly imagine how it went, and of course the bright colors quickly disappeared.

When my boy cousins became teens, they all had cell phones, but if they viewed something that wasn't up to the high standards of the Duggar rules, as a form of punishment the offending iPhone would be quickly replaced with an old-school flip phone for months at a time.

Bill Gothard taught his followers to avoid "eye traps," anything that could entice a male to lust. My uncle and aunt came up with a way to protect their children: The word *Nike* wasn't just a brand of shoe; it became a code. If the family were out in public and the older girls or parents saw something they deemed inappropriate, they'd say, "Nike," and immediately all heads went down in unison. No one was allowed to look up until the all clear was given.

I was about eight years old when I first noticed how quickly all the kids obeyed, never stepping out of line. *Whoa*, I thought, *that's impressive, and somewhat crazy.*

This kind of constant vigilance became a way of life for my cousins that was ingrained in them from a very young age.

Music of any kind with an offbeat drum was considered ungodly and forbidden, as was dancing, and only hymns and classical music were allowed in the home or vehicles. Even praise and worship music was considered ungodly, following the lead of Bill Gothard, who teaches that rock music, regardless of lyrical content, is inherently evil. My cousins' family took this to the extreme, with batteries removed from musical toys so as not to encourage toddlers and babies to dance. Most television shows were considered to be of the devil, so things like Saturday morning cartoons and Nick at Nite programming were forbidden. And don't even think about suggesting going to a movie in a movie theater.

As a young girl, I remember seeing all my cousins listening to the radio, as if we were back in the days of black-and-white television. It was evident how eager they were to learn more about the world they were sheltered from. On shopping trips to Walmart with my aunt and cousins, we'd pass by televisions that were airing kids animated movies, and after we left, they asked me questions like, "Amy, what happens at the end of that movie?" You could sense their deep longing to connect and fit in with the outside world.

The idea of Santa Claus was considered satanic; even the youngest children, at just two years old, would refer to him as "Satan Claus." They were completely shielded from all Christmas movies—no *Elf*, *The Grinch*, *A Christmas Story*, or even *Rudolph the Red-Nosed Reindeer*. While I agree that Christmas has a deeper meaning and that people can sometimes get carried away, it's hard to imagine never experiencing the magic of Christmas-themed entertainment as a child. A little fun is harmless! Trick-or-treating and harvest festivals were also off-limits. Instead, my cousins would decorate for Christmas on Halloween night. They never knew about the tooth fairy or the Easter bunny either.

Movies and television shows were strictly regulated too. Anything that showed emotions like anger, annoyance, sadness, confusion, or even silly slapstick humor was banned. My aunt and uncle believed these emotions could lead to bad behaviors or even an attraction to the opposite sex, which was seen as something to be avoided at all costs until their father thought they were the appropriate age for marriage.

What about Disney films like *Cinderella*? Off-limits. She was defiant and didn't honor her stepmother. Also, the fairy godmother was magical, and the animals talked.

Once I tried to introduce my cousins to *VeggieTales*, a cartoon series featuring silly singing vegetables that taught morals and Bible lessons. I thought surely my uncle would approve of the kids seeing it, but I was wrong. "Amy, take this sinfulness out of my house. I don't want my children to think that vegetables can talk," he said in all seriousness.

Each day, everyone was homeschooled for hours, and the kids

were taught to never question authority, but to always respond with, "Yes, ma'am" and "Yes, sir." My uncle and aunt demanded "instant obedience" as the correct response to any question or command from an authority figure. No one ever yelled, no one was ever irritated, and nothing but kindness was tolerated.

As a girl who loved her cousins and looked up to her uncle Jim Bob and aunt Michelle, I didn't think any of this was weird, because these laws, rules, definitions, and jurisdictions didn't just suddenly appear one day; the decorative posters bearing the strict rules had always been there, even in the closets and bathrooms. The Duggar family environment was a well-oiled machine, designed to instill discipline and order. Everything had a place and a purpose, and like little robots, each child knew their role in the family unit.

Reinforcing traditional gender roles, the boys were encouraged to pursue work and expected to lead their own families in the future. They were taught leadership skills and prepared to be future heads of households with a strong emphasis on learning a trade or profession to become the family provider. Boys were groomed to take on leadership roles in the church and community, with an emphasis on authority and responsibility. The young men were not allowed to work for any big corporation or in jobs where there were women present. They were taught that the world is filled with worldly women, including at college, and this would disrupt the calling God has on your life, so college was to be avoided. Instead, my cousins have worked in a family business setting, started a lawn care business, or worked in the automotive industry. My uncle is the unquestioned leader of the household, and he made all decisions about who his kids could be around, even in the work world.

I had to carefully watch what I said in their house, and I didn't even cuss! Words like *golly, geez, dumb, gosh, darn it,* or *crud* were off-limits. Saying something with a strong emotion like, "I hate tomatoes," was not allowed. All words had to always be as sweet as honeycomb. Other rules included:

no eye-rolling
no mean looks
no slamming doors or being aggravated
no teasing each other
no secrets

Emotions were always to be kept in check. The only emotions allowed were ones that honored the Lord, and anger certainly wasn't one of them.

Even with all the rules, it's no wonder I loved to be at my cousins' house. My own home was vastly different. I had to deal with more than just my parents' fights; I had to deal with my grandpa Duggar too.

CHAPTER
THREE

Grandpa Duggar

Grandpa Duggar was a complicated man. His name was Jimmy Lee, although he went by the nickname JL. He was off-the-wall, unpredictable, reckless, and practically a real-life Kramer from *Seinfeld*. He was the life of the party, the one who could make anyone crack a smile with his antics—such as slurping Jello through a straw.

JL lived on Mountain Dew and sweet tea. He hated aquariums and would sing as loudly as he wanted to, whenever he wanted to. He laughed during serious events and often made a scene. He always had old caramels in his pocket. He wore an Arkansas Razorbacks hat every single day. He was claustrophobic, and he couldn't figure out how to go up an escalator (if you are picturing the movie *Elf*, that is exactly what he looked like). He used old newspapers as toilet paper (don't ask me how I know that). He had zero etiquette at restaurants and would walk into the kitchen and get his own chips or refill his cup. I still don't know how he got away with that! He once ordered and paid for two hundred red plastic cups at a Chinese restaurant and then loaded them into his trunk. Why? No one knows. A classic gag: Gramps would park his car at a fast-food place and literally walk up to the speaker outside and order, then still on foot he'd act like he was driving an imaginary car and growl loudly, pretending to rev his engine.

Grandpa was not only hilarious but possibly a little insane. He was loud and boisterous and unfiltered, possessing a special brand of zaniness that made it impossible to ignore. You never knew what he was going to do next. He put ketchup on everything, and I mean everything, including cereal and ice cream. He loved to play chess every chance he could, and he could sell anything to anyone. At least this was the grandpa I grew up knowing and these are the memories I kept in my head.

But who in the world was Jimmy Lee Duggar, really? Because along with the fun and laughter came a much darker side. This is the million-dollar question, friends, and let me tell you, the answer is about as clear as mud, even though he was my own flesh and blood, married to my grandma Mary, and father to my mom, Deanna, and to her only sibling, Jim Bob.

Even though Grandpa made all my cousins and me laugh, we learned by the time we were in junior high to be very cautious around him. I'm not sure exactly when it happened or why, but eventually there were certain boundaries put in place by my mom and my grandma. There was a shift in our family where the things we thought were funny suddenly weren't funny anymore. Gramps had a crazy side, and we all knew it, but we didn't fully know yet his darker side.

After countless years of speculation and wondering why those safeguards were put in place, I uncovered pieces of the puzzle that began to reveal glimpses of a larger picture. I don't claim to have all the answers to who he really was and what he did, but I have some. After some serious research and talking to folks who knew him back in the day, I began to get answers. The things I found out made me cringe—secrets no one has known or shared until now. But to tell the whole story, I'll go back to the beginning of JL's life—in his own words, the "dusty dirt roads and good ole days."

Childhood was a traumatic experience for JL. His father battled alcoholism and had a very violent temper, often using his son as a punching bag. Gramps's mother, Velma, would on a whim hop on a bus and leave her four kids for weeks at a time to escape her husband's wrath, seemingly not caring about the impact her absence had on her young children. For much of his childhood and young adolescence, JL found himself seeking stability elsewhere. I've been told he used to break into homes when he was younger, commit vandalism, and steal items, only to sell them again. He was never caught.

He and his siblings found refuge in his grandparents' home, where they were doted on, spoiled rotten, and shielded from responsibility. JL grew accustomed to getting whatever he wanted without facing any consequences. The lack of structure and discipline in his life set the stage for a troubled adulthood. As JL grew up, his reckless spending became a defining trait. He had a particular fondness for purchasing run-down used cars, often without considering the long-term financial consequences. After he married my grandma, his poor financial choices led his own family into a cycle of instability, where making ends meet was a constant struggle. The breaking point came when Jimmy was arrested for fraudulent dealings in a car transaction, leading to a ninety-day stint behind bars.

During Grandpa Duggar's incarceration, he fell into a deep depression, further distancing himself from the responsibilities of family life. With her husband absent, my grandmother was forced to step up in a way she never expected to. She took charge, not only of their home, but also of their financial future. She worked tirelessly at a local yogurt shop, becoming the primary breadwinner for the family. My grandmother's resilience was nothing short of extraordinary as she balanced caring for their two children—my mom, Deanna, and my uncle Jim Bob—while managing the day-to-day challenges of her husband's absence.

Despite the overwhelming difficulties, Grandma never wavered in her commitment to provide for her family. Recognizing the importance of securing a stable future, she dedicated herself to learning and improving her skills. She studied relentlessly and ultimately found success in the world of finance. Through sheer determination, she became a real estate broker and eventually founded her own company, Good Neighbor Realty. Her hard work paid off, and the company thrived. The legacy of her perseverance lives on today, as Good Neighbor Realty continues to operate, now run by one of my cousins.

Worse than my grandpa's poor financial choices was his penchant for other women. He was a six-foot-two, blue-eyed charmer who was silly and fun. He was also a serial cheater, and his infidelity was a constant strain on his marriage to my grandma. To this day, I don't know how many affairs he had. One affair was particularly hard on Grandma. It was with a woman who lived just under an hour away and led to a six-month separation when my mom was only six years old. During that time, Gramps never came home to see his two children, though he would call them on the phone. When he eventually returned, Grandma forgave him, acting as though nothing had happened. Life continued on, and she never spoke of it again. Nor did she ever address the deep wounds he had caused.

Despite the pain and distance between them, my grandparents decided to dive into the hotel business together. They took on ownership and management of the Rest Haven and Iris Motels in Fayetteville, Arkansas. The motels were basic, one-story white buildings along Highway 71, with the Duggar realty company right next door. My mom's great-grandparents' house sat right behind the motels. The five-acre property was farm-like and covered in trees.

The family lived in the attached apartment that came with the office, and Grandma took great care in keeping the properties clean and well-maintained. But though the businesses provided them with a steady stream of cash, the influx of money did little to heal the rift in their marriage. Instead of bringing Grandpa and Grandma closer, the venture only added to the tension between them. They were caught in a constant power struggle, and their fighting was relentless. Their arguments played out in front of my mom and Uncle Jim Bob, creating an atmosphere of instability and unresolved conflict. It was clear that, despite the outward appearance of success, their marriage remained deeply fractured, with no real resolution in sight.

Grandpa's obsession with used cars never wavered. Even when the family's finances were already stretched thin, he would continue to sell anything he could get his hands on, from household items to cherished pets, just to fuel his latest obsession. It was as though he didn't know how to be an adult, struggling to manage responsibilities and make choices that would provide stability for his family. Instead, he sold off anything that wasn't nailed down—including my mom's beloved Airedales, Mitzy and Kristy. Those dogs weren't just her pets; they were family. But to my grandpa, they were just another means for making a quick buck, with no thought for the heartbreak he caused or the lasting impact of his choices. We often joked that he could sell flip-flops to an Eskimo, a testament to his skills as a salesman. But his knack for getting a deal didn't seem to extend to understanding what truly mattered—his family's well-being.

When things didn't go his way, Grandpa didn't accept it quietly. He made sure everyone knew about it. He had a flair for drama and would throw himself into tantrums, cussing, hollering, and carrying on. My mom often told me stories about growing up in a household where out-of-control behavior was a regular part of their lives. She witnessed her parents' fights night after night, sometimes stretching into the early morning hours, the arguments escalating like a heavyweight boxing match. Words would fly like punches, and tempers would flare hotter than a Southern barbecue.

The atmosphere in the house was charged with tension, full of emotional turmoil and unresolved conflicts. The constant fighting created a toxic environment that affected everyone living there, including my mom and my uncle. For all the material things they managed to obtain, material success never brought peace or stability. Instead, the Duggar household was a battlefield where love and respect seemed to get lost in the chaos and where emotional wounds were inflicted just as often as they were ignored. It was clear that what he really couldn't be sold on was the idea of taking responsibility or building a future with integrity.

My grandma tried to protect her children in her own way, and she put up a boundary where JL wasn't allowed to be alone with his daughter. She did the best she could, but despite her boundaries and best efforts, JL's relationship with his daughter was particularly fractured and strained. He rarely called her by her real name, instead choosing most often to call her "Cow." He knew the nickname hurt her, and it was a cruel, deliberate way to strip her of her dignity, leaving her feeling ashamed, unloved, and unworthy.

Her father's cruelty didn't stop at name-calling. He took pleasure in mocking the scars on her legs, scars that were earned from climbing trees and playing outside to escape the constant yelling and chaos inside the house. Those scars on her legs were reminders of her attempts to find some peace, but they became ammunition for his taunts, and he would make fun of them every chance he got. Jimmy Lee seemed to thrive on tearing people down, constantly poking at their vulnerabilities, and my mom took the brunt of it.

Emotionally, Grandpa Duggar was hardly there—unless his temper took over. When he did show up, it wasn't with warmth or care; it was with anger and harsh words that left lasting wounds. He had a habit of making big promises he never intended to keep—family vacations that never happened, the dream car he swore he'd buy for my mom, even the small things like ballet classes she longed for or karate lessons for Uncle Jim Bob. He'd say all the right things, make them believe, then let it all fall apart. Over and over again, his words meant nothing. The disappointment became a pattern they learned to expect. His emotional neglect and abusive behavior were a constant source of pain and contributed heavily to the dysfunction that plagued our family.

To make matters worse, my grandparents subscribed to a harsh and controlling way of raising children. They believed in corporal punishment and used whatever was within arm's reach—whether it was a hairbrush, a belt, a paddle, or a wooden spoon. There was little distinction between discipline and cruelty, and the line was often crossed. These physical punishments were meant to instill fear, but what they truly instilled was a deep sense of shame and a broken relationship between parent and child.

Despite the chaos my grandpa stirred up, my grandma did love my mom in her own way. She threw herself into supporting my mom's dreams, chauffeuring her to piano and voice lessons. And my mom continued to win pageants and singing competitions. Somewhere along the way, her parents developed an unrealistic expectation that my mom was destined for stardom. No matter the cost, no matter the turmoil, they were determined to make it happen. "Don't help me bake cinnamon rolls in the kitchen," Grandma would say. "Go work on your singing." They were sure she would be a big star. While they were busy chasing their own dreams of being stage parents, they failed to see the wreckage they were causing at home. My mom's potential stardom became the lens through which they viewed their lives—this picture-perfect idea of success—while the foundation around them was slowly crumbling. Sound familiar?

My mom often talks about her brother, Jim Bob, and how he was reserved, withdrawn, and shy growing up. He never sought the spotlight and always tried to stay out of the way, content to keep a low profile. He was a good kid—an extremely kind and loving brother.

Deanna and Jim Bob were very close, sharing a stacked bunk bed until their teen years when they finally had their own bedrooms. My mom, the protective sister, would watch over him during the turbulent times when their parents fought. In those moments, they'd either huddle together for comfort or run outside to escape the chaos. Through it all, my grandma did her best to create a sense of normalcy and give her children a good childhood, even though the circumstances were far from ideal.

But a shadow far worse than her dad's cruelty loomed over my mom as she got older, when she realized why she was never allowed to be alone with her own father.

CHAPTER
FOUR

Grandpa's Shadow

Mom never really thought much about why she wasn't allowed to be alone with her dad. It had always been the norm, so she never questioned it.

But when my mom was in her early twenties, she finally understood. One evening while Grandma was in the back of the house, JL was lying down in his bedroom. He suddenly called out for his daughter, his voice demanding. As she approached his bedroom, her heart began to race with a mixture of apprehension and uncertainty. She knew something was off.

When she opened the door, she was met with a request no daughter should ever hear from her father. In a serious tone, JL said, "Deanna, I want some special time with my daughter." His words dripped with an unsettling intensity. "Why don't you come and lie down with me?"

To this day my mom can still remember his lustful eyes, her dad patting the bedsheets as he spoke. The evilest thing of all was his sickening smile. My mom's instincts kicked into overdrive, and without a second thought, she slammed the door shut and fled from the room.

The incident was never discussed.

From that point on, my mom knew there was a much deeper, uglier, and sadistic side to her father. She never took a shower if he was home, and she locked her bedroom door at night. It was an awful way to live. She liked to invite friends over to swim in the pool, but eventually she stopped inviting them because JL would try to flirt with them and chase them around the pool. About five years ago, a customer came into my store and told me a shocking story: A neighbor of Grandma's told her that when this woman was a teen, Grandpa would grope her at the pool, pull down her bathing suit bottoms when no one else was around, and have his way with her. My grandma brushed off the story and told the neighbor she was lying and just wanted attention.

And that was the last time that event was discussed.

Throughout the years, several women came forward with similar stories of how my grandfather flirted with them and forced himself on them. Church women's tongues were wagging with the many rumors of JL's infidelity in and around our small town. My grandma brushed off the comments every time. But the truth is that, as I mentioned previously, JL Duggar was not a faithful husband, and sometimes he wouldn't come home for days at a time. Though my grandma was quick to dismiss any story about him, the evidence against him was clear. I've heard from several trustworthy people who knew him that he slept with multiple, and I mean *multiple*, women.

As typically happens in the Duggar family, despite these unfortunate events, life marched on. My mom was under the oppressive thumb of her father and yearned for independence. She was twenty and desperate for a place to call her own, where she could finally escape the suffocating grip of her father. She set her sights on getting her own apartment, determined to break free from the toxic cycle that had ensnared her for far too long. However, just when she thought she was on the brink of freedom, her parents swooped in with their own brand of persuasion. With arguments laced with warnings, they painted a picture of doom and gloom, convincing her that leaving the nest without a wedding ring was not the godly thing to do. If she chose to leave, she would suffer both worldly and eternal consequences.

Fear became their weapon of choice as they whispered lies and doubts into her ears. They made her believe that disaster would surely strike if she dared to venture out on her own, away from the supposed safety of her parents' guidance. She felt completely trapped. Even though she wanted so badly to leave, fear held her back. Their codependency was too strong to resist. So she stayed with her parents—afraid and uncertain, feeling as though escape was just out of reach.

In the fall of 1980, my mom went to John Brown University with the goal of singing in a select music group called Joy Song. She auditioned, beat out forty-nine other girls, and won a coveted full-tuition scholarship. Although she loved the social aspect of college, the academic life wasn't for her, so she left college after a year and a half to pursue her dreams in the music industry.

The day she returned home from college, she walked into the living room and found her dad yelling violently at her mom. Although this was the type of behavior my mom had always known, something felt different this time. JL apparently was under severe financial stress, and the tension in the air felt heavy. He seemed dangerous. But because Grandma seemed to be handling him in her normal feisty way, my mom brushed it off, assuming it was just another argument that would eventually fade. She quickly left the living room without saying a word to her parents and went to her bedroom, hoping to escape the weight of it all, and began unpacking.

But her father followed my mother, storming into her bedroom. With a leather belt in his hand and the most haunting, crazed look in his eyes, he grabbed her by the legs, held her down on the bed, and began beating her, every hit harder than the last. She fought to break free, but he overpowered her. He was six foot two and, although slim, was very strong. This brutal torture lasted for more than an hour. She screamed at the top of her lungs for help, begging him to stop, but the lashes continued, and she began to bleed.

When Mom was black-and-blue and beaten to a bloody pulp, eventually the torture stopped, and JL left the room, too worn-out to keep going. My mom knew that getting out of the house was of utmost importance. She worried that at any moment her father would come back to finish what he had started. That night she saw her opportunity. She very quietly opened the window, hoisted herself up and wriggled out of it, then started running as fast as she possibly could—running toward help, relief, and freedom.

My mom made it to a neighbor's house down the road. Fortunately, they were home and able to help treat her wounds. They urged her to call the police and report this abuse from her father, but fear held her back. She was terrified of what he might do if she reported him, afraid he'd come after her with even more rage, maybe even try to kill her if she dared to expose the truth.

One thing that has always stood out to me when my mom tells this story is that throughout the entire horrifying event, the one thing that hurt worse than the beating and every rage-fueled lash from her dad was that while she was screaming for help, crying, pleading for him to stop, begging for her life, her mother never came to help.

Never came to her rescue.

Never came to save her.

Never spoke of it or acknowledged it.

Another incident took place later, when my mom was a young twenty-one-year-old and in love for the first time. She went to tell her parents, as most people do, that she had met someone special, the man who would later become my dad. She was scared to tell my grandparents she wanted to move in with him, knowing they believed that living with a significant other without first getting married was a huge sin. When she did tell them, her worst fears were realized. JL went ballistic again. He grabbed her by the throat, carried her from the kitchen to his bed, and jumped on top of her. He wrapped his hands around her neck, lay on top of her so she was unable to move, and started strangling her. She gasped for air, unable to scream or yell. Grandpa shouted at her, "I'm going to kill you, Deanna!" He almost succeeded in murdering my mother.

Right when all hope seemed lost, Grandma called Jim Bob in a panic. He walked into the bedroom and saw what was happening. "Dad, what are you doing? Get off my sister!" This pulled JL out of his fit of rage and he let go of my mom.

Jim Bob might not have known it at the time, but he saved her life that day. And just like the time when JL beat my mom with a belt, my grandma was in the house, never lifting a finger to help her, never saving her, never rushing to her rescue. And never speaking of it again.

You would think that after yet another traumatic experience like this, my mom would never want to go back to her parents' house again. However, narcissistic people know how to use fear to control their victims. My grandpa knew how to manage his words. He apologized and manipulated his way back into Mom's life and convinced her not to press charges. Again. Even my grandma told my mom not to get carried away, telling her how bad it would look for my grandpa because of his previous time served for fraud. My grandparents successfully convinced my mom that things would be different going forward, and that it was in her best interest to continue to live there. The physical abuse did stop. But the bickering and name-calling never did. He still called her Cow and never showed my mom even an ounce of respect.

While I didn't know any of these stories when I was young, as I look back, I recall understanding the unspoken, nonnegotiable rule that seemed to hang in the air like a heavy fog: *Never be alone with Grandpa*. It was as clear as day. Grandpa couldn't be trusted. I knew to obey that rule, innately understanding that breaking the rule would have very bad consequences.

When my grandparents came to live with my mom and me because my dad's violent threats became too scary for my mom to handle on her own, I was given clear rules: Grandpa Duggar could never take me to school, never join me in the backyard for a game of catch, and absolutely never be allowed to come into my room. My grandma checked every single night to make sure I had locked my bedroom door before going to bed. "If you hear Grandpa in the middle of the night, do not hang out with him," she said.

I couldn't sit with him on the couch and watch a movie; I couldn't be alone with him in a car; and I couldn't practice my cheerleading routines in the living room or wear a bathing suit to sunbathe outside. I couldn't even play Barbies in front of him because my grandma didn't want me to risk showing him their naked bodies. Above all, I could not under any circumstance step foot into his bedroom or take a bath or shower unless my grandma was home. I wasn't allowed to have friends hang out, and sleepovers were strictly off-limits.

When I was in my teens, I wondered why Grandpa spent so many days in bed. He reminded me of the grandpa in *Willy Wonka & the Chocolate Factory*, and I speculated that he might have an underlying illness or was just lazy, because sometimes I wouldn't see him for days at a time.

It all seemed so strange at the time, but I accepted the rule without question, simply because that's how things were. In hindsight, I'm astounded by how unaware I was. Just like my mom's experience in her childhood, I repeatedly heard so much yelling and fighting coming from my grandparents' bedroom that it would keep me up at night. I heard Grandpa call Grandma every name in the book. I witnessed several physical fights between them. I once saw my grandpa slap my grandma in the face on a road trip, and then my grandma punched him hard in the face and tried to grab the steering wheel from him, all while I was sitting quietly in the back seat.

They would often try to control my mom, causing her to fight back, and shouting would echo through every room. Phones were hurled against walls, TV remotes shattered, and doors slammed.

I would hear my mom crying all the time, which broke my heart. I'd lock my bedroom door, turn up the volume on my music, and try to drown it all out. I remember shaking in my bed when I was little and thinking, *One day, it won't be like this.*

Although my mom did her best to try to protect me from all the chaos, she couldn't keep me safe all the time. Many days, Grandpa left me with painful welts from the random times he would hit my legs with switches torn from the maple tree in our front yard. The blows hurt, and I didn't understand what I did to deserve the pain. I would cry, but he'd show no mercy. "Crying is for the weak," he would say.

One time, I was home in the middle of the day playing outside by myself. The ball I was playing with rolled into the street. The wind carried it farther and farther down the road. My only thought was to catch it before it got too far, so I ran down the street after it. Just then my grandpa turned onto our street and must have seen me. I heard the engine of his maroon Ford Mustang coming up close behind me. My stomach clenched as I realized he was coming up way too fast. I turned my head just in time to see him barreling toward me. As I ran, the thought hit me: *This man is a lunatic.* I ran down the street, zig-zagging to get away from him, and finally took a hard right turn into my neighbor's bushes. I stayed outside until dinnertime, too afraid to go anywhere near him. His actions had always been unpredictable and oftentimes abusive, but never before had I been scared for my life the way I was that day.

Grandpa Duggar often left me feeling desperately confused and hurt, but I didn't cry. I grew up believing that crying was a sign of weakness, something to be ashamed of, exactly like he taught me to believe. To shed tears felt like exposing a vulnerability I wasn't supposed to show. I didn't want anyone to see me as fragile or incapable; I wanted to be the strong one, someone who could handle anything that came my way. Admitting to pain, fear, or heartache felt like admitting defeat. So I held it all in, bottling it up.

Grandpa could also be kind in ways that left me feeling conflicted. He'd compliment me unexpectedly, making me feel seen in those fleeting moments, or go out of his way to thaw my car's windshield on a bitter winter morning. It was as if he thought these small acts of kindness could make up for his intense, volatile behavior.

At the time, I thought this kind of fear, brought about by emotional and physical abuse, happened to all kids. I didn't realize that children should feel safe, cherished, and nurtured at all times. I didn't realize that the abuse I was experiencing was anything but normal. It wasn't until much later in life that the reasons behind those strict restrictions with Grandpa began to truly make sense.

CHAPTER
FIVE

Silent Shields

After my grandparents passed, my mom and I sat down and had a long and deep discussion. She broke down and told me the stories she has given me permission to share with you. I remember the moment it all clicked for me: The reason I was not allowed to be alone with my grandpa was because he was a *predator*!

Underneath JL's charming and funny personality was a true monster. He wanted to hurt me, and he wanted to hurt anyone he could when given the chance. Grandma, bless her soul, felt like my silent guardian angel quietly watching over me. Despite her best efforts to shield me from harm, I still endured a lot of pain because of him.

My grandma never spoke a word to me about what she endured at the hands of my grandfather or if she had a sense of remorse for the moments when she couldn't safeguard my mother from severe abuse. However, I believe she was determined to break the cycle when I was born. I believe she was striving to provide the nurturing and protective environment she wished she had created for her own daughter. Ultimately, she failed at protecting my mom, so Grandma did everything in her power to protect me in the best ways she could.

Imagine if I had left my door unlocked one night. She knew my grandpa and what he was capable of. Every night, without fail, she would diligently check the lock on my door in a small yet meaningful gesture that demonstrated her commitment to my safety. Similarly, her unwavering presence in my daily life was evident as she faithfully picked me up from school each day, providing not only practical support but also a comforting sense of stability.

Perhaps most telling was her decision to include me in her real estate showings, a measure taken to ensure I was never left alone in the company of my grandpa. This felt like her deliberate way to try to shield me from an abuser. She prioritized my protection above all else. Grandma was someone I could rely on. And despite her faults, she was my best friend.

I think because my grandma helped raise me her heart softened, or maybe her mind changed or her perspective shifted, to see me more like a second daughter than a granddaughter. Maybe she was taking hold of a second chance—this time, she would do the right thing. She would try to instill the values she held so dear and protect the ones she loved.

And then there's my mom. She is my fiercest advocate. And a true holy disruptor.

A true warrior in every sense of the word, my mother's strength and resilience shaped the very foundation of my life. Deanna Duggar's battles began long before I was born, and through it all, she remained steadfast in her resolve to protect me from the dangers she knew too well. She worked long hours and sometimes worked the night shift as a receptionist in the emergency department at our local hospital, sacrificing her sleep to make sure I had everything I needed. During the day, my grandma stepped in, offering me a safe haven while my mom worked tirelessly behind the scenes.

Every day after school, Grandma would pick me up and take me to McDonald's for my usual—a plain cheeseburger and an apple pie. Then we'd head to the thrift stores, never in a rush to get home. I think she knew I needed that time, just the two of us. She made the smallest things feel important, asking about my day like it truly mattered, listening to every detail, even the petty stuff. She never brushed me off, never made me feel silly for what I cared about. And when it came to homework, she was right there beside me, patient and encouraging.

Those afternoons weren't just routine; they were little pockets of love, a safe place in the middle of mayhem. I didn't realize how much they both gave up for me or how hard they fought for my future and my protection. But looking back, I'm overwhelmed with gratitude. The weight of their bravery, strength, and selflessness is something I carry with me every day.

Grandma and Mom were silent protectors, yes. But their actions spoke louder than any words ever could. Because of them, I'm here today, protecting my son and setting boundaries in my own life because of what these two women did for me. They were holy disruptors for me, passing their strength on to me.

The first time my mom shared her past with me and told me about the abuse she had endured, my heart plummeted like a stone sinking into a deep lake. The weight of the truth was massively heavy. I couldn't hold back the flood of tears as I witnessed my mom remembering these horrible stories. In every single one, I felt like I took on the burden of my mother's pain. I held her hand as it shook and hugged her tight. I didn't want to let go. My mom is a survivor, but it broke my heart that someone I loved so deeply had experienced such unimaginable pain and suffering.

The cycle of inherited trauma that began with my great-grandparents continued its relentless journey through the generations. It impacted my mother and Uncle Jim Bob and eventually made its way to me and my cousins. But family is a confusing dynamic. Though my grandpa inflicted pain on so many people, he was still so lovable. We had so many inside jokes. I laughed every time he grabbed a ketchup bottle to put it on every food item he had. I liked how playful he was, always joking around.

But still I wonder, *What caused this person I knew so well to be so evil? Who might have abused Jimmy Lee? How many others did Jimmy Lee abuse?*

I'm not sure I will ever know the full answer.

Hurt and pain breed more hurt and pain. And unless we actively work to heal the brokenness within us, the pattern of hurt and pain affects every aspect of our life and the lives of those around us. Unresolved issues only perpetuate it, rolling out like an avalanche of poison onto future generations. This cycle persists until someone dares to disrupt it—dares to become a holy disruptor who acts as a force for healing and change.

> Hurt and pain breed more hurt and pain. And unless we actively work to heal the brokenness within us, the pattern of hurt and pain affects every aspect of our life and the lives of those around us.

My family's culture of secrecy fostered an environment of denial and suppression, where hard truths were never spoken of in favor of maintaining a facade of normalcy. Deanna and her brother, Jim Bob, learned at a very young age how to hide their pain and shame behind closed doors and how to shield outsiders from knowing the truth. Telling the truth, in the face of bad news, was frowned on because the situation did not align with what was deemed acceptable to the outside world. The expectation was that we would always keep private matters private. It didn't matter what the truth was; our appearance, our standing in the community mattered most. I know my grandma knew about my grandpa's many infidelities. I think she simply decided to ignore it and stuff it as far down as she could.

Not once was any fight ever talked through with me. No one ever pulled me aside to explain what happened or why things had escalated the way they did. There were never any apologies—not for the yelling, not for the fear it caused, and certainly not for how it made me feel small and unsafe in my own home. I was just expected to move on as if nothing had happened.

But kids *deserve* apologies. They deserve to know that their emotions matter and that adults are capable of owning their mistakes. An apology doesn't erase the pain, but it helps heal it. It teaches a child that conflict can be repaired and that relationships are worth mending. When we skip that step, we teach kids that love is conditional and that accountability doesn't apply to everyone.

As I mentioned earlier, my grandpa's father had an insane temper, in addition to being an abuser of alcohol. JL must have learned at a very young age how to seize control through his temper, how to treat women poorly, how to manipulate people, and how to get away with bad, even criminal, behavior. The recurring list of unhealthy and disturbing behavior goes on and on, all part of a vicious cycle—one that my family has never been able to truly escape. Generational trauma continues when there is an inability to tell the truth . . . and the truth has *always* been hidden in our family.

It's a puzzle I've struggled with. Was Grandma living in denial, or was she too trusting, too inclined to see the best in people? What kind of abuse did she endure? Those who dared to confront her were rejected, and what they had to say fell on deaf ears. How could anyone, especially a parent, not protect their own daughter? It seemed like nothing, even fear of her own husband, could shake her unwavering belief in the sanctity of marriage. Now doesn't that sound familiar?

Let me tell you, what you saw from my grandparents on the television screen was a far cry from the truth. My grandparents paraded their love in public like it was something to be envied and celebrated, but behind closed doors, there was no love lost. Their marriage was a battleground, a constant tug-of-war between two souls who had long lost sight of what it meant to truly love and respect each other. They weren't the best of friends, not by a long shot. Beneath the public-facing facade of marital bliss lay a deep-seated resentment, a festering wound that neither of them dared to address. It was as if they were trapped in a cage of their own making. And let's not mince words here—I'm convinced that deep down, they harbored a seething hatred for each other. But in public, their emotions were hidden behind smiles, and they pretended to be shiny happy people.

Why do people do the things they do? It's like we're all carrying around these bags full of curses and traits and patterns passed down through the generations, each one shaping who we are and how we navigate the world. But what exactly is a generational curse? Here's my take: Once upon a time, someone in our family tree—maybe a great-grandparent, maybe even further down the line—adopted a belief or a pattern of behavior. It may have been something they thought might protect them, something that made sense in the context of their pain or fear. But instead of the belief or behavior ending with them, it took root. It became a part of the family's unspoken rules, passed down like an old heirloom.

And over time it embeds itself so deep into our lineage that we don't even recognize it as something that doesn't belong there. We just carry it unknowingly until someone finally decides to break the cycle. These curses—these unhealthy cycles—have a way of weaving themselves into the very DNA of our lives, and unrecognized by us, they shape our thoughts, beliefs, and behaviors. Until we take a good, hard look and confront these trauma patterns head-on, they'll just keep on repeating themselves, spreading like wildfire to our kids and their kids after them.

But we don't have to be slaves to our family history. We have the power to break free from these chains, to stand up and fight against the tides of negativity and dysfunction. Just because my grandpa used to pick up twigs and hit me with them doesn't mean I'll *ever* pick up a twig and hit my child. Absolutely not. The cycle of abuse ends with me. I've broken free from that legacy of pain.

We are not bound by the actions or choices of others. Each person must bear the weight of their own decisions; we are not meant to carry the burden of mistakes we didn't make. What we can do—what I've done—is look deep within and work to change the behaviors that have been passed down. We have the power to choose to create something new.

When I was younger, I would ask myself, *What kind of future do I want? Who do I want to be associated with? What are the things I will not tolerate in my life anymore? What generational traits am I ready to defeat?* Taking a stand hasn't been easy, but I have made a deliberate choice to break free from the generational curses that have waged war against me. I've dug deep within myself, rolled up my sleeves, and taken responsibility for my own healing. Those toxic behaviors— whether they were manipulative, predatory, or rooted in denial—no longer have a place in my heart or my life. Narcissism, physical abuse, and fear have been expelled from my garden of life, and I refuse to let them have any power over my future or the future of my son.

I know I'm not the only one to face a battle like this. I'm sure some of you reading this have faced or are facing similar battles in your own family. I want to encourage you to take a hard look at your own life. Do you have weeds growing in your garden—destructive patterns, unhealthy behaviors, or toxic influences that have held you back and kept you from thriving? It's time to start digging. You have the power to change your present and your future for the better. You can be the hero of your own story, the one who sets a new course for your family's future. By doing the hard work now, you can pave the way for a brighter, more peaceful tomorrow for the generations that will come after you. Don't wait for someone else to fix it. Be the change your family needs. The time to heal is now, and it starts with you.

> You have the power to change your present and your future for the better.

Disrupt.

CHAPTER
SIX

The Parent Trap

You may be surprised, given what you just read about my grandfather and my mother, to hear that these next two chapters were, without a doubt, the hardest ones to write. It wasn't the act of writing that was difficult; no, it was that these chapters are deeply personal, and putting these words down feels like baring a part of myself that I've kept hidden for a long time. This is a part of my story that has to be told. Up to this point, I haven't had the courage to tell it.

Raise your hand if you have daddy issues. Or a parent complex. If you've been hurt by someone who was meant to protect you, then you are not alone. I see you, and I share the same pain. How tragic it is that some men and women fail to step up and embrace the role of being a parent! When someone brings a child into this world and then doesn't fulfill their obligation to love them, it leaves a void that is hard to fill. Whether a parent was emotionally unavailable, had high expectations that the child couldn't meet, or was crushed under the weight of their own unresolved hurt and baggage, the result is that unhealthy and absent parents place an unfair emotional burden on the child.

Whatever circumstance you may have gone through with your

parents, if you were neglected or felt unloved or unaccepted by them, I'm sending you a huge hug right now. I know that heartache is not easy to heal from. When I was younger, I felt deeply insignificant to my parents at times. Parents should be our greatest protectors and nurturers. I spent years trying to have a relationship with my dad. Fathers are supposed to be our first heroes, the ones who show us what love and security feel like. They're meant to be the solid ground we can stand on, their unwavering presence assuring us that everything will be okay. But what happens when that ground gives way? It is heartbreaking and difficult for me to reconcile the two sides of my dad—the sometimes-loving father from my childhood and the source of my deepest wounds.

My mom met my dad at a Christian bookstore when she was twenty-one. I know, it sounds like the setup for a sweet, faith-based love story, but trust me, their whirlwind romance was more like a rom-com that turned into a cautionary tale halfway through. From the outside, their story looked like a match made in heaven, with two young people bonding over their faith and shared love of Christian cassette tapes (because, yes, that was the era when tapes were still a thing). When my mom met my dad, she thought she had found true love. He was the answer to her prayers—literally. He was always talking about God, and he seemed genuine and full of devotion.

It was the perfect setup, everything my mom hoped for—a God-fearing man who would honor her, love her, and fill the emotional void she had lived with for so long. He was her knight in shining armor who was going to carry her away from the abuse she endured in her parents' home. She was young and hopeful, and more than a little eager to escape the emotional chaos. The two quickly became inseparable. Mom was convinced she had found her person—someone who wouldn't turn into her father. But from the start there were cracks in the foundation. Mom had such a desperate need for love, security, and validation that she ignored the red flags flying in plain sight.

Just nine months into their relationship, my mom found out she was pregnant.

With me.

She was still practically a kid herself, and while she had dreams of having a family, she had no idea how to handle the reality of it, especially when her relationship with my dad was built on emotional dependence rather than on mutual support. Their love was very new and hadn't been tested or shaped by real communication, respect, or stability.

When someone has unresolved daddy issues, they often look to romantic partners to fill the emotional void. My mom wasn't just looking for a husband; she was looking for a savior. The catch is, when you're driven by that kind of emotional neediness, you don't always choose the healthiest partners; you choose the one who seems like they're ready and available to fix your hurt.

My mom had never truly addressed the abusive relationship with her father. So when she fell for my dad, she was chasing the idea of healing without realizing that no man, no matter how seemingly godly or charming, could give her what she needed most—self-love and emotional healing. The truth is, no partner can "fix" you, especially when you're carrying baggage from childhood that hasn't been unpacked. My mom didn't realize it then, but what she really needed wasn't a romantic hero; she needed to confront the abuse, abandonment, and emotional neglect she had experienced.

So there she was at twenty-two, pregnant and emotionally unprepared for the realities of life as a mother and a partner. On September 30, 1986, I came into the world. It was anything but celebratory. My grandma later told me a story about that day that broke my heart. According to her, after my delivery, my grandparents were in the hospital room when my dad came in. He walked over to my mom and whispered, "I should have killed you and the baby while I had the chance."

I can't imagine how painful that must have been for my mom to hear. There she was, holding her precious newborn after having just given birth, and at the very moment when everything should feel right in the world, the person she had conceived this child with had only cruel and heartbreaking words to say. My grandpa and my dad wound up in a huge fight and punches were thrown. Hospital staff called the police, who came and escorted my dad out of the hospital.

My mom tried to move on from my dad after he spewed those horrific, ugly words in the hospital. Her parents were only too happy that their fast-moving, volatile relationship was over. But it wasn't long before my dad sent her flowers and a love note, and they were right back in each other's arms.

But things didn't go according to her plans. Eventually, the strain of their mismatched expectations took its toll, and my mom, tired and heartbroken, broke up with him, leaving her all alone, with the help of my grandma, to raise me.

CHAPTER
SEVEN
Fire Meets Gasoline

Due to the severity of my dad's anger issues, I wasn't allowed to see him for the next two years. My parents kept their distance from each other, rarely talking, and my dad only occasionally connecting with me. But inevitably, through my dad's persistence, my mom and dad got back together. Again. This time they were determined to make their relationship stronger and healthier than before. I was six years old and couldn't wait to have him back in my life. I dreamed of finally being a real family. I'd missed him a lot and quickly forgave him for his past mistakes. My dad seemed to have genuinely changed.

Though my mom and I still lived with my grandparents and Dad had his own place, he took a lot more interest in my life for the next several years. I remember vividly the good times we had throughout my childhood. I loved our endless summer days by the pool, when my dad made it seem like the season would never end. He always surprised me with a new bathing suit every year! We'd swing for hours under a tall oak tree, my feet reaching the lower branches. We saved turtles crossing the highway and spent our Saturdays canoeing on the

Elk River. We'd cheer together for our favorite college baseball team at every game. And at night, after the dinner dishes were cleared away, we'd play endless rounds of Uno. Somehow I always seemed to win.

Dad introduced me to classic rock and the enduring quality of Levi Strauss jeans. He loved to paint and encouraged me to embrace my own artistic side. His creative spirit was infectious. He had a knack for introducing me to new experiences, taking me to local jazz festivals and antique stores in nearby towns. He also taught me valuable life lessons, like how to care for my things, respect everything around me, be on time, and always be polite. He emphasized the importance of generosity, especially in the form of tipping well, showing me that kindness and gratitude should always be shared with others and that hard work pays off. He worked at a plastics company for more than twenty-five years, where he was loyal and well-respected. He had a magnetic charm that drew people in, and all my friends adored him. Life with Dad could be wonderful at times, but it could also be dark, depending on how my parents' relationship was going. And I found myself having to tiptoe around my dad, not disagreeing with him for fear that he would become angry and yell at me for hours.

My mom and I would often drive thirty minutes to my dad's house to spend Saturday and Sunday with him. Whenever we arrived, the atmosphere was charged with passionate kisses or intense arguments—there was no middle ground.

At times, I felt like we were a real family, enjoying normal moments together around town, including attending worship services together at a little church in my dad's town. But there were also times as a little girl when I'd walk into the living room to find them cuddling on the couch and feel a pang of exclusion, thinking, *There's no room for me here.* I would pass the time by playing with neighborhood kids or retreating to the back room to watch Nickelodeon for hours. With no one to supervise me or limit what I watched, I would flip through channels, watching whatever caught my eye. I certainly lacked guidance and protection during those formative years.

My parents were too busy trying to figure out how to be in a relationship. Together, they were like fire and gasoline—volatile and explosive. Though individually they had many admirable qualities I respect, together they seemed to add fuel to each other's worst traits. My parents' relationship was an emotional battleground, with an unhealthy and chaotic intensity that spilled over into every aspect of our lives.

Their fights were not just occasional tiffs; they were drawn-out fights that could last for hours on the phone. My mom, for good reason, was filled with mistrust and anxiety, so she would secretly drive the thirty minutes to my dad's house, desperately searching for any signs of another woman in his life. Meanwhile, my dad would call our house phone relentlessly throughout the night, checking to see if he could catch my mom with other men, often escalating their arguments by shouting death threats. On the phone my mom would hang up on him for what seemed like fifty times, but he'd call right back. He was relentless.

When my parents fought, it always started with raised voices, but it never stayed there. The tension would build until my dad was full-on screaming at my mom, and she'd be crying so hard she could barely speak. But he wouldn't stop.

I frequently found myself in the middle of their emotional cross fire. My dad could be incredibly affectionate and attentive one moment and then suddenly transform into someone cold and distant the next. His affection was erratic, a weapon used to manipulate and punish my mom. One day, he would shower me with love-bombing gestures— poems filled with adoration, proclamations of how I was the light of his life and the perfect daughter, or unexpected outings for shopping. These moments were intoxicating, but they were also fleeting. The very next day, his demeanor would change abruptly. He'd emotionally withdraw, refusing to give me a hug or engage with me, leaving me in a state of confusion and hurt. His affection felt like something to be earned rather than given. The inconsistency left me feeling as though I had to constantly prove my worth.

I learned early on never to cross my dad. Beneath his charm and occasional kindness, he was an unpredictable and volatile man. His temper was like a ticking time bomb, ready to explode at any moment. When he was angry, he would yell and curse, and his rage was so intense that he would break things or throw things into the fire. I'm not just speaking metaphorically; he would actually destroy things in the heat of the moment in a fire he kept smoldering in a metal trash can outside. He used it daily, not only to burn trash, but to burn anything near him when his temper flared—dinner scraps, plates, napkins, clothing, pretty much anything in his line of sight.

Growing up, I believed I was the problem. He certainly made that belief ring true for me. In his fits of rage, Dad would belittle me, saying I didn't have a brain cell left in my head and calling me names. His discipline was extreme, including throwing my favorite cereal into a tree, grabbing me by the neck, throwing me against the wall for not brushing my teeth, destroying my closet because I used wire hangers instead of plastic (maybe a childhood trigger I know nothing about), or tossing my *Lion King* handheld video game out of the car window because he didn't like the sound it made.

My mom wasn't spared either. If she made him mad, he would take scissors to her favorite dresses, berate her, or lock us out of the car and drive off, leaving us stranded, no matter how far away from home we were. He ruined many holidays with well-timed outbursts to maintain his control. We were ridiculed nonstop. My mom couldn't think clearly. She said my dad was just temperamental, not abusive, although it was clear she was scared of him. She loved him despite how he mistreated us. He knew how badly she wanted to marry him, and he dangled that possibility in front of her like bait—just enough to keep her holding on, only to snatch it away whenever it suited him. Their relationship felt like walking through a minefield, where one wrong step could trigger an explosion. While my mom and dad seemed to enjoy the chase, I desperately wished the games would stop, and I was left feeling like collateral damage.

His fists never physically touched me, but the emotional blows from my dad were awful. Each painful word cut deeper than the last. He never missed a chance to hurl venom my way when he was angry, and I can still hear his cruel words:

"You'll never amount to anything."
"I have never loved you."
"No one will ever love you."
"What a waste of a life you are."
"You should find a career where you just lie down on your back
  and take it."

The weight of his venomous words continues to haunt me. Those words broke me back then, and even all these decades later, that last comment still stings in its raw ugliness.

I learned early on that my opinions didn't matter. Any time I dared to express myself, it was like shouting into a void, where nothing comes back but mockery and dismissal. I began to always agree with my dad for the sake of not being yelled at. He'd laugh at my spoken thoughts or cut them down until I stopped speaking altogether. Silence became my shield, though it was a fragile one, and deep inside I felt like I was disappearing.

Being gaslighted and demeaned for so long erodes our self-esteem to the point that we no longer trust our own thoughts or emotions.

Every time my feelings were hurt, I'd swallow the pain, knowing the script of his go-to line all too well: "Well, if you were a better daughter . . ." It was his favorite poisonous dart aimed directly at my heart. If not that, he'd retreat into icy silence, a withdrawal so punishing that it made me feel invisible, like my existence truly didn't matter.

My bedroom became both a sanctuary and a prison. It was the only place where I could hide from my dad's relentless verbal abuse, but it was also a space where the echoes of his words reverberated, sometimes more loudly than when he had spoken them. Inside the little world of my room, I wrestled with myself, wondering why my own father didn't love me and why I wasn't enough. I knew, somewhere deep down, that Jesus loved me. But in those moments, that truth didn't feel accessible. How could I believe in divine love when the person who was supposed to love me unconditionally, the one person who should have seen my worth, made me feel so utterly worthless? How could I be worthy of God's love when I wasn't even worthy of my father's?

For twenty-five-plus years my mom fought, pleaded, and begged for my dad's love, hoping that something would change. We both tried everything. We changed ourselves, adjusted to his moods, and did whatever we thought might finally be "enough." But no matter what we did, it never was. His approval was always out of reach.

Their toxic relationship consumed my mom. It pulled her into a deep depression that became a constant shadow in our lives. Her anxiety spiraled out of control, and she could barely function under the weight of it all. She was drowning, and I was powerless to save her, no matter how hard I tried. When things got unbearable and my dad's threats worsened, she asked my Duggar grandparents to move in with us. She wanted my grandpa there for protection, even though he had been awful to her. It was a desperate move, asking the very people who were part of the history of abusing my mother to protect her. My grandpa literally hated my dad and had never accepted him, so he was more than happy to move in.

Our home was clean and welcoming, at least when only my mom and I lived there. But when my grandparents moved in, our home quickly became a chaotic mess, like something out of the show *Hoarders*. Grandma Duggar was unable to let anything go. Old magazines, chipped plates, broken appliances—nothing ever found its way to the trash. Every corner of the house was piled high with clutter, teetering towers of forgotten items that served no purpose but to take up space and collect dust. My grandpa never bothered to pick up after himself. He'd leave newspapers scattered across the living room—a trail marking every place he had been.

I liked order and tried to keep my room as clean as I could. But no one ever cleaned the rest of the house, and soon we weren't the only ones living in the overwhelming and disgusting mess. Mice began to take up residence, drawn by the food crumbs. I remember lying in terror listening to them scurry through the walls at night, the unwelcome sounds echoing through the stillness. One morning before school, I saw a mouse in my room and watched it as it ran across my feet. I've hated them ever since.

The bathroom was the worst. Black mold grew unchecked inside the bathroom cabinet, and we had to tape it shut because the sight was too unbearable. Mold spread like a dark cancer through the room, an ugly reminder of the neglect that permeated every part of our lives. The house was honestly unlivable, yet somehow we lived in it. I dreaded anyone coming to the door, fearful that someone might see inside and judge us or, worse yet, pity us. I often heard my mom and grandparents yelling at each other about my dad and what my mom, as a grown woman, was allowed to do. When my grandparents moved in, the house became a battleground where they fought with my mom over control of her life.

I found myself scared and uncertain about what was really happening, so I would hide in my closet, covering my ears and singing to drown it all out. Surrounded by clothes, I felt a strange sense of safety in that tiny space. On the occasions I got out of the house, I met my friends by the fence or took my pillow and blanket outside to sleep on the trampoline. *One day I won't live like this*, I'd think to myself while gazing up at the night sky. I'd stare at the stars, shaking, praying for the chaos to stop.

My mom has always called me the tree that shaded her because of the way I've looked out for her and tried to protect her since the time I was a little girl. I cherished that nickname, but despite my efforts to help her and act as her unlicensed therapist, any advice I offered about coping without my dad only seemed to deepen her depression. I missed her so deeply, even when we were just steps apart in the same house. She fell deeper and deeper into despair, her laughter fading and the light in her eyes going dim. Each day, I could feel her drifting away from me, and I had no idea how to bring her back.

Every day after school, I slowly opened my mom's door, bracing myself for the familiar sight of mascara-stained tissues piled atop her floral bedspread. Her tiny bedroom was crowded with clothes stacked high in the corner, a nightstand coated in thick dust, and chocolate wrappers scattered on the floor. It was a sad, stagnant scene. She spent so much time in bed and hardly ever went outside, as if the weight of her world kept her from moving beyond the four walls of that room. I remember sneaking my Barbies into her room, hoping to sit on the floor beside her just to feel her presence, even if she wasn't truly there.

I missed my mom so much, even when she was right in front of me. I just wanted my mom back—the one who smiled easily and made everything feel okay. Her presence had once been my safe haven, but that comfort now felt distant. As a child, all I longed for was her acknowledgment, embrace, and reassurance that everything would be all right. But she was trapped in her own pain, and as much as I needed her, she couldn't be there for me the way I desperately needed her to be. Instead, she was fixated on my dad.

There were still fleeting moments of happiness when Mom would smile, bake cookies, and take me shopping, usually when things were going well with my dad. It felt like she was trying, like she wanted to create happy memories with me despite everything weighing her down. Birthdays were her way to make me feel special, and even though my dad never financially contributed to our daily living, he would pay for my parties. Those celebrations felt like magic in the middle of the crazy. I was too young to realize that these grand gestures always came with strings. But even on those days, the shadow of drama always loomed. Having everyone together in the same room was like walking on a tightrope. I was always on edge and wondering when the next fight between my grandpa and dad would break out.

During my early teen years, everything shifted even more. I felt like I couldn't bring my mom any of my own problems. I knew she'd understand heartbreak, confusion, and the challenges of growing up, but she was already drowning in her own sorrows. How could I possibly ask her to carry my burdens too? Her life seemed to be endlessly filled with pain, and I didn't want to add another thing for her to think about. It broke my heart to see her struggle. I wanted so badly to save her, but I didn't know how. All I could do was watch helplessly as her depression kept pulling her further away from me.

There were days I desperately needed her guidance and comfort, but I learned to go on without it, even though I was left feeling hollow. With my mom battling depression and my dad's inconsistent presence in my life, I began to seek love elsewhere—or at least what I thought was love. Burdened by hurt and insecurity, I fell hard for a blue-eyed bad boy, and our tumultuous relationship lasted five long, unhealthy years. Unfortunately, it seemed like history would repeat itself, and I would follow in the footsteps of my parents. My boyfriend cheated on me repeatedly, yet I found myself giving him one chance too many, influenced by what I had witnessed with my parents. I was in love, but he wasn't, and I learned the hard way that words mean nothing without actions to back them up. His betrayal left me feeling manipulated and heartbroken.

Even through all the madness and years of strife, my mom still clung to the crazy idea that my dad was the one for her. My dad continued to convince my mom he had truly changed. He started going to church regularly and spoke of how deeply sorry he was for all the pain he had caused her over the years. He made it seem like he had turned a corner, and for the first time, he seemed genuinely remorseful for the heartache and chaos he had brought into our lives. They began talking about going to counseling, which they had avoided doing in the past. They even started praying together, and for those few months, my mom truly believed she was witnessing a life transformation.

That transformation lasted about six months. During that short time, my dad became the man she had always wanted him to be. He listened to her. He was present, and for the first time, it seemed like he genuinely wanted to be committed—not just to her but to the idea of being a husband and having a real family. My mom, who longed for this kind of love and partnership, began to trust in that change. It wasn't just that he said all the right things; he started showing up in the ways she had always dreamed of. He made promises to her that he seemed to be keeping. At age fifty-two, my mom finally saw a version of my dad she had never seen before, and for the first time in a long while, her heart was filled with hope.

She believed, deep down, that this, finally, was the man she had fallen in love with all those years earlier—the one she always knew was hiding beneath the surface of the mistakes and manipulation. She clung to that belief. And for a brief golden moment, it felt like they were moving in the right direction, like maybe their prayers and hard conversations were finally paying off. For the first time, they had something in their relationship that resembled peace. On September 14, 2006, my parents finally got married. I was nineteen years old. The wedding took place in a small, intimate ceremony in Eureka Springs, Arkansas, and my mom was such a beautiful bride. Holding purple roses on a sunny afternoon, my mom was filled with a hopeful glow that seemed to light up the whole day.

For a moment, I let myself believe that maybe this was the new beginning we all desperately needed. *Maybe now we can finally leave the pain behind and be a loving family*, I remember thinking. I was hopeful, but painfully naive.

EIGHT

Leaving College Behind

Most people on the cusp of becoming a legal adult can't wait to escape the suffocating grip of their parents' house and launch out on their own, embracing their new freedom and the thrill of choosing their own life.

That wasn't me; I didn't dream of getting away.

I spent my entire childhood yearning for something different, something many kids take for granted—a real family and a stable home, like my uncle Jim Bob provided for my cousins. When my mom and dad got back together and walked down the aisle to say their wedding vows, it felt like my last chance at that cherished dream. So instead of leaving, I made the decision to move into my dad's house along with my mom. I thought, maybe, if I stayed, I could help protect her if things started going badly. That instinct to shield her, to take on her burdens, has been with me since I was a little girl.

But despite my reservations about leaving her alone with my dad, my mom insisted I give college a try. She reminded me I'd never get this time back, reassured me not to worry about her, and promised she would keep herself safe by spending a lot of time with Grandma. I reluctantly agreed.

Following my boyfriend—the one who continually cheated on me—I enrolled at Southwest Baptist University in Bolivar, Missouri. In a way I felt like I was leaving my mom behind, so I packed my bags with some regret. Then I gave my mom a huge hug and left.

This was a different path from that of my cousins, who weren't allowed to go to college, so I decided to take the opportunity to learn and grow. Grandma always supported whatever I did and gave me her vote of approval. My dad didn't seem to care much one way or the other about my enrollment because he still had control over my mom. Uncle Jim Bob didn't approve, of course, and when he learned of my plans, he told my mom that college might not be a good idea for me: "It isn't a godly choice."

College became a haven for me. I loved it. I was now a legal adult, and I realized I had other dreams beyond being part of a safe and loving family. Armed with a college education, maybe I could become a therapist, a newscaster, or, the really wild career, a storm chaser. I majored in communications, and I loved psychology and meteorology. I started making real friends and loved keeping a schedule filled with classes and lots of college activities.

But the weight of my parents' issues continued to loom over me, a low-level storm that made it difficult to concentrate in class.

I'll never forget the frantic call I got from my grandma's phone one night while I was studying for an exam. It was late in the evening, and I picked up, expecting to hear Grandma's steady, familiar voice that always calmed my heart and made me feel safe and warm. But instead, it was my mom on the other end, her voice shaky and full of fear. "Amy," she whispered, "it isn't good."

I could tell right away she was crying. There was a pause, and my heart pounded as I listened to her catch her breath. Then she said, "He's not happy with me. He took my shoes, my purse, my keys to the car . . . even my phone. I had to run to the gas station down the road to get away from him. I don't know what he's capable of, Amy. I'm so scared."

A chill went through me as I processed what she was saying. My mom, who was always so strong and composed, was terrified. She had to flee barefoot from her home. I pictured her, desperate and vulnerable, trying to reach someone, anyone, who could offer comfort or guidance.

Here I was, a hundred miles away, tied to my college dorm room by exams and assignments, powerless to do anything for her.

That phone call changed everything. I took a deep breath and made a decision: *I cannot allow this*. Nothing else mattered more than my mom's safety. I couldn't stand the thought of her feeling so alone, so helpless, with no one to protect her. My mom needed me.

After I found out that Mom was safe for the moment at Grandma's house, I packed my bags, dropped out of my classes, and took a moment to hug my roommates and say goodbye to everyone in the dorm. I kissed my boyfriend goodbye and told him college just wasn't for me, although I wasn't telling the truth. We tried to make it work, but the distance only exposed what I didn't want to admit: He was partying, drinking, and pulling away. I kept hoping he'd change, hoping we'd find our way back. But then one weekend, he came home, and I went to surprise him only to find him in his bedroom with another girl!

That was it. My first love wrecked me. I had never known that level of betrayal before. It cut me in a way I didn't know was possible. But as painful as it was, it pushed me to search for something better, something healthier. That heartbreak became the turning point that made me realize I deserved more.

It felt surreal, leaving behind the new life I had just started to build, but I didn't look back. I drove the three hours to my grandma's house, and when I finally got there, I held my mom as tightly as

I could. I wanted to let her know she wasn't alone. We spent a week with my grandma to give time for my dad to cool down. It seemed to work. He called my mom, apologizing that he flew off the handle and promising to try harder to be the man she deserved. Though it was a sliver of a belief, it felt like maybe, just maybe, things would be different this time.

A brief honeymoon phase ensued where my dad once again really did seem different. He was attentive and affectionate, and for a moment, our three intertwined lives felt seminormal. But slowly, the familiar cracks began to show again, and the glow of hope that had sustained us in those early months started to fade. My dad's temper, which had always lurked just beneath the surface, began to creep back in. At first, it was small things—an irritated comment here, a frustrated sigh there. But soon those little moments of anger grew into the familiar fiery storms that none of us could predict. My heart was always in my throat.

His anger couldn't be contained inside the house; it followed us everywhere. I'll never forget the countless times when we were driving and my mom didn't make a turn fast enough or the music wasn't to his liking. Without warning, he'd fling open the car door, threatening to jump out while we were speeding down the highway at seventy-five miles per hour. Dangling halfway out of the car, Dad would scream at us while the wind whipped through the open door. His behavior scared us half to death, and my mom's hands would grip the steering wheel, white-knuckled, trying to keep control of the car and the situation. I always sat frozen in the back seat, trying not to cry and praying he wouldn't jump, that we wouldn't lose him.

Sundays, a day of rest reserved for the Lord, were no better. If we lingered too long after church, talking to friends or simply catching our breath, we ended up frantically searching for him because he would disappear without a word, leaving us to scour the building and parking lot. We'd drive around aimlessly, hoping to spot him. Eventually we'd find him stomping down some remote country back road, Bible in hand, furious that we hadn't followed his unspoken schedule. It didn't matter if it was blistering hot or freezing cold; he would walk for miles. Mom and I would pull up beside him, pleading with him to get in the car, but his face was etched with anger and his silence louder than any outburst. We knew that once he was in the car, there would be repercussions.

The craziest thing about my dad's behavior was that he knew the Bible inside and out. He could quote Scripture effortlessly, and he proudly adorned our home with religious paintings and framed Bible verses. Yet the life he led was the exact opposite of the teachings about a Christlike life he supposedly believed. The Bible says, "By their fruit you will recognize them" (Matthew 7:16), implying that true followers of Christ should naturally embody qualities like "love, joy, peace, forbearance, kindness, goodness, faithfulness, gentleness and self-control" (Galatians 5:22–23).

Behind closed doors, my father's "fruit" was bitter and corrupt, his actions steeped in manipulation and anger and a far cry from the love and compassion he declared. The difference between his public persona and his private behavior was crushing. The man who should have been a spiritual leader was instead a symbol of everything I feared in a future life partner. I could feel his anger in every part of my body, mind, and heart. It filled the room, the air, the house, and my world.

Dad hated my mom's cooking, and no matter how hard she tried, nothing she made was ever good enough. He called her every name imaginable, tearing her down over a burnt corner of bread or a meal that wasn't seasoned to his liking. One time, she burned some eggs, and I remember him flinging open the refrigerator, pulling out the egg container, and throwing away all the eggs in it. He grabbed the spatula and broke it, then tore the dishrag to shreds. Lastly, he picked up the pan, stomped outside, and threw it into his ever-smoldering metal trash can.

My mom and I both knew he could be set off at any moment, and I watched her tremble in the kitchen, her hands shaky as she tried to prepare meals, knowing that no matter how carefully she made the food, it would never be right in his eyes. It amazed me that she could still boil water with how nervous he made her. To ease her burden I started cooking, hoping that maybe if I messed something up, he wouldn't lash out at my mom.

I hated every second of it—the powerlessness, unfairness, and constant fear. I wanted to scream at him and tell him to stop, but I was trapped in my own silence, still trying to protect her in whatever little ways I could. I would find things to do in my room to keep busy, trying to drown out the sound of his voice, to push down the anger and heartache. He loathed everything about my mom—her hair, her clothes, her makeup. He'd ridicule her about her weight and made her weigh herself on a scale. He reveled in tearing her down in every way possible.

We would gather as a family to watch a movie when suddenly he'd start pacing the room, his anger building with every step. His eyes would narrow into a furious glare directed at my mom, and just like that, the evening would be over. To ensure our safety, we'd have to leave. Her purse and our shoes were kept close to the door, so we could be ready for a quick exit. We learned to dart out of the house with practiced precision, like a drill, knowing we wouldn't be safe again until we were far from home. I can't even begin to count the number of times we left the house in fear and panic, desperate to escape my dad's wrath.

One time, my mom was so furious with my dad that we packed up and left. Instead of heading to my cousins' house or a friend's place, we decided to treat ourselves to one of the nicest hotels around. We had the best girls night—just the two of us. We ordered room service; slipped into big, fluffy robes; and had a movie marathon. It was exactly the pick-me-up we needed after a huge fight had erupted. Sometimes we just needed to escape and create a little bit of joy for ourselves, even if only for a single night.

But like the unpredictable weather systems I dreamed of chasing, I never knew when the next bad day with my dad would come. I vividly remember the first time I saw everything my mom owned strewn across the front yard. *What in the world happened?*

I rushed into their bedroom, only to find her side of the closet completely demolished. Empty hangers lay scattered on the floor. Dresser drawers were wide-open and empty; all of her clothing, including intimate apparel, now filthy, was scattered throughout the yard, fully exposed to the neighbors and to the elements. Her cherished sweaters were covered in dead grass, her jewelry scattered across the lawn like sad confetti after a celebration gone wrong.

My dad had already left for work and my mom was out of town, leaving me to face the aftermath of his inexplicable behavior. Despite my desire to escape this continuing nightmare, I canceled everything I had planned to do that day, grabbed trash bags, and began the painstaking process of picking up every single item from the cold ground. Each sweater I retrieved was soaked in dew and dirt, a clear sign of how long it had been left there. Each piece of jewelry was tarnished.

I spent hours washing and fluffing the clothes, hanging them up again in the closet, and meticulously reorganizing my mom's jewelry armoire. It was a grueling, exhausting process, and touching each item broke my heart over and over again. I was driven by a desperate need to restore some semblance of order and her dignity. By the time my mom walked through the front door, no one would have known a tornado had torn through our home.

After that first time, whenever my mom was out of town, I woke up, only to look out the window to see everything she owned strewn across the front yard yet again. A chaotic jumble of her personal treasures had been discarded again overnight as though they were trash. When my dad came home, he acted as if nothing had ever happened.

I never breathed a word about these incidents. Seeing my mom's things thrown out like that became my silent burden. I carried that secret alone, and it weighed heavily on my heart. I knew the real devastation was not in the belongings scattered across the lawn but in the secrets I was carrying. I was consumed by the knowledge that if the truth came to light, it wouldn't just be heartbreaking; it would shatter my mom's fragile world. I wanted so badly to protect her from all the pain. This cycle was a repetitive ordeal, one I endured in silence far more times than I care to remember. I knew my mom loved my father no matter what he continued to do to her, and in my mind, it had become my sacred duty to shield her from the worst of it for as long as I could.

CHAPTER
NINE

Saying Yes to Actual True Love

I never went out much, but one night I needed a break from the crazy and went with my friends to a local bar. I needed to feel young, hear some live music, and have fun for a change. On that particular night, I met a guy named Dillon. Yep, we met in a bar! Dillon was a friend of a friend, and you could tell right away that he was hilarious, full of life, and had a flair for the dramatic. I had heard his name come up a few times before I actually met him, so when he walked up and introduced himself, I already knew who he was.

I expected Dillon to throw out some kind of pickup line, but instead, he *insulted* me! He looked me up and down and said, "What the heck are you wearing?" Now, to be fair, this was during the era when shirts covered in ruffles were all the rage, and I also happened to have on colorful feather earrings. He didn't hold back and said with a sparkle in his eye, "You look like a peacock!"

Most girls would've been totally put off. But honestly, I found it refreshing. Here was a guy who wasn't trying to hit on me or impress me at all; he was just being himself. I laughed, surprised and amused. And then he smiled and said, "I'm Dillon. Let's go get a drink."

We ended up exchanging phone numbers, and from that moment on, we became best friends. It was purely platonic, but we spent a lot of time together, always laughing and sharing inside jokes. We clicked right away, but only as friends. He was a ladies' man, definitely not boyfriend material, and I wasn't really attracted to him when we first met. So without hesitation, we both placed the other in the friend zone. Over the course of six years, we built a strong, unshakable friendship, never crossing any boundaries.

One afternoon, Dillon called me, his voice bubbling with excitement, and invited me to hang out with some of our mutual friends. Over the years, his voice had increasingly become a light in my stressful world. But this time, I had to decline his invitation. My mom was out of town, and I was busy putting our house back together. My dad would regularly tear apart the house before he left for work, a shocking act of violent control. My mom was always in intense pain because of her knees, but we would work tirelessly all day to make the house sparkle by the time he got home. The fighting never ended about the housework and the chores.

Trying to stifle my tears and on the verge of breaking down, I told Dillon I couldn't go. Dillon heard the sadness in my voice and asked what was wrong. I was too overwhelmed to fully explain, but it was clear to him that I was not okay.

Twenty minutes later, the doorbell rang. I opened it to see Dillon standing there. I could only imagine what he thought when he saw me. I looked like I hadn't slept in days, my eyes swollen and teary. I had a big pimple on my chin, and my T-shirt had dirt smeared on it. I smelled like a public restroom, and my hair was a mess. Dillon was seeing me at my absolute worst, but without a hint of judgment, he pulled me into a tight hug. I was so relieved to see him. I cried as he held me, and I broke down and told him about my living situation. He listened, offering comfort and understanding. For the first time in what felt like ages, I didn't feel so desperately alone.

Then he followed all that with an unexpected offer: "Well, if you have to stay home and clean, you don't have to do it alone!"

I wanted to cry again. Here was a friend who genuinely cared, who picked up a rag and started dusting and then vacuumed the floors while I put away the laundry. We did dishes together, waxed the leather sofa, and made the house shine. He was willing to stand by me, even in my messiest and most vulnerable moment. Dillon was becoming the only person I trusted enough to confide in, and he called me every single day to check in. Every time we talked, those minutes on the phone turned to hours of long conversations. Sometimes the yelling between my parents was so bad that I'd call Dillon late at night and find out that he couldn't sleep either. We talked and talked, and then when I started to get sleepy, he stayed on the phone with me until I fell asleep. I know—*swoon!*

One night at a local bonfire, Dillon showed up with another girl, which completely threw me off. Normally, I'd be the first to give her a warm hug and make his new friend feel welcome. But this time, my first thought was that she wore too much eyeliner and shouldn't be wearing Dillon's jacket. And I didn't like her name. I wasn't about to let him know how I felt, though, so my friend and I decided to leave the party early. All the way home and well into the night, I kept venting about Dillon bringing this girl to the bonfire. We sat in the hot tub, and I just couldn't let it go.

Finally, my friend looked at me and said, "Amy, you're annoyed because, deep down, you like him!"

I remember laughing. "Oh, I'm going to need a glass of wine for *this* conversation!" But as we talked, it started to sink in—she was right. I *did* have feelings for him. Still, the fear of getting my heart broken was enough to keep me quiet. So I decided to stay silent, hiding what I'd just come to realize.

I've never been good at hiding my feelings or keeping a poker face. The more Dillon and I texted, the more obvious my feelings became. Before long, I wouldn't even bother hanging out with our friend group unless I knew he'd be there, so I'm sure it didn't take a genius to figure out the one my heart was tilting toward.

One night, Dillon invited a bunch of us to his place, and I might have strategically picked out a short skirt for the occasion. *Wink, wink.* We all sat around talking in the living room, but at one point, I went into the kitchen. When I turned around, there he was. He had followed me.

Now I'm not saying I was drinking a lot, but that night, Dillon and I had a little liquid courage. We were standing close, talking quietly, when out of nowhere he leaned in close, looked straight into my eyes, and kissed me. Then without missing a beat, he whispered, "When I look at you, I see forever. I want my life to have you in it, and I want us to have a family together." After that, let's just say we kissed a little more—no shame! I drove home that night feeling like my whole world had just shifted in the best way possible. I was full of hope. *Maybe this is the beginning of something real and lasting.*

The next day, Dillon called me and casually asked, "Wanna grab lunch?"

I hesitated, not wanting things to get awkward. "Sure, but I just don't want things to get . . . weird between us, you know? I mean, everything you said was a lot."

"Huh? What did I say?" His voice was neutral.

I was *dumbfounded*! How could he not remember what he had said, with the whole "forever" and "family" thing?

Scrambling, I stammered, "Oh, d-don't worry about it; it's nothing really." Inside, though, I was left wondering, *Was it the alcohol talking, or did he really mean it?*

After that, I played it cool, calm, and casual, and for more than a month, Dillon kept asking me what he had said that night, but I wouldn't tell him. He sent me random texts, saying, "Just tell me!" but I stayed stubbornly silent. Then one day, he called, sounding frustrated. "Amy," he said, "not knowing what I said to you is *killing* me. Please just tell me."

So I finally told him. But the moment I said the word *forever*, he hung up on me!

I sat there, thinking, *Well, I definitely freaked him out. I'm not calling him back after that.*

A week passed, an entire week of total silence, which felt like forever in texting terms. But the next Friday, out of nowhere came a knock at my door. When I opened it, there stood Dillon, with one hand on the doorframe, looking nervous and shuffling his feet.

He looked up at me. "You know, when I really think about it, it *is* you I want."

And then we kissed. This time he remembered.

We decided to give dating a try, but shifting from a close platonic friendship to a romantic relationship was more challenging than I expected. We weren't quite sure how to navigate the change. I approached things cautiously, carrying wounds from past relationships in which I had been cheated on and deeply hurt. Dillon, on the other hand, hadn't been in a serious relationship in five years, so this was all new to him too, and he was rusty.

Our biggest struggle was communication. I'd call him after not seeing or hearing from him for days, telling him, "I miss you," and he'd respond with, "Why?" When we were just friends, he was great at calling and texting, but now that we were in a new relationship, it felt like there was pressure. Even though we cared about each other, we were both holding back, maybe afraid of letting each other in too fully. And without strong communication, our relationship was on shaky ground. Eventually, it became clear we couldn't keep going like that.

I kept myself busy with fun nanny jobs. I needed a break from Arkansas, so I jumped at the chance to vacation in Florida with one of the families I nannied for and brought a friend along. During the day, we had a blast building sandcastles with the kids and playing in the ocean, but when they were tucked in bed at night, we went out and explored the nightlife. My friend happened to have some friends in the area, and one evening we went out dancing. That's when I was introduced to a blue-eyed heartthrob who made me forget my own name. The only problem was, I had a boyfriend, and I'm loyal to a fault. But once I was back from my trip, Dillon and I broke up. On the romantic side, the split wasn't too painful; I missed Dillon as my friend more than anything. It was tough going even a single day without hearing his voice. If only we could figure out how to blend friendship and love.

I didn't stay single for long. Mr. Florida turned out to be a pretty good thing, and we dated for about six months. He was going through a divorce, had a daughter, and had definitely lived a lot of life. Part of me thought, *If Dillon doesn't love me enough to be with me, I'll just find love somewhere else.* I think, deep down, I was so eager to find my "forever" that I tried to force it, but there were a lot of obstacles with this new boyfriend. For one, he lived in Florida and I lived in Arkansas. Plus, as fate would have it, my uncle Jim Bob knew his ex-wife's family (small world), and she had moved back to live in Arkansas with their daughter.

One day, Uncle Jim Bob called me and announced that if I didn't end things with this guy, he would make sure I'd never have a chance at any television opportunities again. I felt completely cornered. *What should I do? Being with someone shouldn't be this hard.* Mr. Florida was going to move to Arkansas to be closer to his daughter, but nobody was rooting for us to be together.

He kept buying me gifts, saying the sweetest things, and pouring out his heart to me. But deep down, I wasn't sure how I truly felt. I wasn't ready to be a stepmom. His words meant so much, but I was still grappling with my own feelings, which were all over the place. I wanted to believe he was sincere, but a part of me wasn't certain. I had to ask myself, *Amy, is this what you really want?* I was deeply confused.

As I was trying to figure out my own mess, I had no idea that Dillon was on his own path, doing some serious soul-searching. For the six months we were apart, he was quietly working on himself. He moved out of a friend's house that had become a bit too chaotic, began focusing on what truly mattered to him, and even started reading the Bible regularly. He threw himself into work, taking on long hours and dedicating himself to figuring out what he really wanted in life. While I was trying to get over someone else, Dillon was transforming himself in ways I never expected.

One day while I was driving down the road talking to Mr. Florida, I got a notification of an email message from Dillon. I quickly pulled over to read it, and what I saw stopped me in my tracks:

> Amy, I'm sorry for the pain I've caused. I've been trying to figure out how I could let the girl I love slip away. The truth is, I'm so in love with you, and I'd jump over any hurdle to be with you. I'll always be there for you, and if you give me another chance, I'll prove it to you. My feelings for you will never go away, and I'm yours forever if you'll have me.

Reading those words caused everything I had been holding back and trying to move on from to rush back in all at once. Dillon's words were so true and heartfelt, and they hit me in a way I wasn't expecting. Suddenly, everything became clearer. I knew then, deep in my heart, that despite the confusion and everything I had been unsure of, Dillon really loved me. I knew where my heart truly belonged. He was everything I had ever wanted.

After that, I told Mr. Florida it was over between us. Dillon and I soon took the leap and began dating again. We called each other and had random dates here and there, but he was always on the move, juggling the relentless demands of owning his own business, and I was trying to keep up with my own busy schedule. Still, we cherished the moments we could steal away together, curious to see how our relationship would evolve. We knew we had something special, and we craved more quality time together.

People sometimes say we should be careful what we pray for, and God certainly had a plan in mind for us. Just as we were getting into the rhythm of our new relationship, life threw us an unexpected curveball. Dillon was involved in a traumatic car accident—a head-on collision with a drunk driver on a slow country road. The impact at 120 miles per hour left him with a shattered femur. It was a miracle he even survived. The months that followed were agonizing for him—with a grueling and painfully slow road to recovery.

But oddly enough, God answered my prayer to have more time with Dillon in a way I never saw coming. My family took off for a trip to Big Sandy, Texas, and with my schedule wide open, I became Dillon's primary caregiver at my mom and dad's house for two whole weeks. I was there for him in his darkest hours, and we suddenly had all the time in the world to truly be together. As I helped him through his recovery, we spent hours talking—about life, our dreams, and our desires for our future. Our relationship deepened during that time, shaped not by the normal pace of dating but by the intense reality of helping someone I loved navigate through pain and healing.

CHAPTER
TEN
Wedding Bells

My dad's violent outbursts were becoming more fre-
quent. I'm not sure if he was upset that I was starting to fall for Dillon
or if he felt he was losing the control he had over me because of the new
man in my life. When I was younger, my dad and I got along well and
had so much fun together. At times he treated me like his little princess,
and yet he still often iced me out. As I got older and had my own views
and thoughts, he became less loving and kind. I was a grown woman
now and not as easy to control anymore. I saw what my mom was deal-
ing with, as I had for years, and I felt stronger and better equipped to
show my true feelings toward him and his behavior.

Whatever the reason, his toxic behavior escalated. One day as my
mom was sitting at the kitchen table enjoying a glass of sweet tea, my
dad stormed in and pulled the chair out from underneath her. My heart
sank as I watched my mom slam to the tile floor, her drink sloshing
everywhere.

He stood there with complete indifference and said with a sneer,
"Deanna, why are you so clumsy?"

I saw the pain and fear in my mom's eyes. I had seen that look
before, and I knew she was silently pleading with me to stay quiet.

She forced a smile, trying to make light of the situation. "I'm not sure what happened. I guess I lost my balance."

I watched them both, horrified.

"Silly me."

Dad stalked out of the house, leaving us to deal with the mess. I rushed to my mom's side, my heart pounding as I helped her up off the floor.

At that moment, I believe my dad was testing the waters, gauging just how far he could push my mom beyond what he had already done to her over the years. Abusers often start subtly, probing for boundaries and observing their victims' reactions. They begin with small, hurtful gestures or verbal jabs to see how much their targets will tolerate. My dad certainly spent decades doing this to my mom. When there's no resistance or when forgiveness comes easily, the abuser is fueled to take things a step further. The boundary pushing becomes a gradual escalation—from emotional manipulation to physical threats to violence. This slow, steady progression allows them to control and wear down their victim bit by bit, until even the most extreme behaviors feel somehow inevitable or inescapable.

One night while he was at our home, Dillon was in unbearable pain. He couldn't sleep or find any relief, and his suffering persisted throughout the night. I was exhausted from staying up with him and desperate for any bit of peace. Just as we were finally settling into the early morning hours to try to get some rest, my dad, an early riser, decided it was the perfect time to make a ruckus. It was four thirty in the morning when we heard pots and pans clanging loudly in the kitchen.

He walked into the living room where we were sleeping and cranked the music on. Already frayed from a sleepless night, I felt like I was on the verge of losing it. *I just can't take it anymore!* I thought.

With every ounce of patience hanging on by a thread, I walked into the kitchen and pleaded, "Shhh, please, Dad. We're all worn-out. We've been up all night, and Dillon needs to rest. Can you please turn off the music and the lights?"

Silence. Instead, my dad walked right past me, eating a sandwich.

A few hours later, I could sense the tension inside my dad continue to rise. He called me into the kitchen. I could feel the weight of the moment before I even entered the room, as if the air was pressing down on me, warning me that something was very wrong. When I stepped into the kitchen, he ordered my mom to take out the trash, a clear excuse to unleash his wrath on me. I met his gaze—hard, intense, and unnerving. The room seemed to close in on me as I stood there. His dark, piercing green eyes turned black as night and locked onto mine. Then he spoke, his chilling words forever seared into my memory:

"This is *my* house, and I'll do whatever I like at any time of day. You *ever* try to hush me again, I'll feed you to a woodchipper. I'll spread your body all over a field where no one can ever find you again! I want to throw you against the wall right now and *break every brittle bone in your body.*"

Paralyzed, unable to move or breathe, my body locked up. My face felt as though it had gone numb, and I couldn't even blink. I was so shaken up that I just stood there in complete panic.

Then I left the kitchen and slowly walked into the living room. I had no idea Dillon had been awake the entire time, silently hearing everything. Our eyes met, and an overwhelming wave of relief washed over me.

Finally, I. Had. A. Witness.

All those times I tried to explain what was happening and all the stories I told him about my dad's behavior were finally validated. Though physically constrained by his injuries, Dillon's presence gave me strength. He couldn't have intervened in the way he may have wanted to, but when I ran over to him, trembling and eyes full of tears, his firm grip on my hand said everything. He looked right at me and whispered in my ear, "You are not staying here. The woman I love will not be treated like this."

Most abusers don't reveal their cruelty when others are watching. They wait until their victims are alone and their defenses down, and the abusers' words can overpower them. They thrive in the shadows, where they can twist reality without fear of being caught.

> Most abusers don't reveal their cruelty when others are watching. They wait until their victims are alone and their defenses down, and the abusers' words can overpower them.

But not this time. Dillon had heard every word, every insult, every threat. He had witnessed the emotional abuse firsthand. For the first time, someone outside of my chaotic world had seen the ugliness I had been trapped in for years, and for the first time I felt safe. Though I didn't quite realize it yet, the burden of facing it alone was no longer mine to carry. Dillon's presence alongside me felt like a shield. He may have been physically weak, but at that moment, he was stronger than ever, comforting me in a way no one ever had before.

As I sat on the couch next to Dillon, who was holding me tightly, we watched in silence as my dad rushed out of the kitchen and through the front door, slamming it behind him with a force that shook the walls. The entire house fell into an unsettling stillness.

Shortly after, my mom walked in and saw the look on my face—pale and still shaken. The tension in the room was thick. The silence in the air felt thick, and without a word being spoken, she seemed to understand.

That moment marked a turning point. I knew I couldn't stay in that environment any longer. I made the decision to move out immediately.

Something changed for my mom that day as well. She started to spend a lot of weekends out of town, visiting friends and spending some nights with my grandma.

From that moment on, Dillon and I began dating with a newfound seriousness. The intensity of everything we had been through together, from his recovery to the emotional ambush of my family, bonded us in a way few couples experience so early on in their relationship. Our bond evolved quickly, and within just eight months, we were engaged.

The way Dillon proposed was like something out of a fairy tale. He mowed down a section of his family's farm, creating a beautiful winding path. As dusk settled in, he lit hundreds of candles along the walkway, the soft glow casting a magical light over everything. The flickering flames danced in the cool evening air, setting the perfect backdrop for what was about to happen.

We walked hand in hand, looking at the pictures he had framed for the occasion lining the path—evoking the laughter, the milestones, the quiet moments we had shared. Dillon spoke softly, nervously, as he recounted the journey we had been on together and how we had come to this point. His words were filled with so much love and sincerity.

As we reached the end of the path, he turned to me, shaking with anticipation. He dropped to one knee, and when he opened the box he was holding in his hand, I gasped. Inside was the ring I had always dreamed of—a stunning oval diamond that seemed to sparkle with every movement. I never told him what I wanted; he just seemed to know. But it wasn't just the ring that took my breath away; it was the man holding it, the man who had been my best friend, my confidant, my love. He was everything I had ever wanted and more. The world seemed to stop, and I knew without a doubt that this was the beginning of our forever.

As our wedding approached, I was faced with a difficult decision—one that weighed heavily on me. Despite everything that had happened, I made the choice to have my dad walk me down the aisle. I struggled with it, knowing our relationship was fraught with tension and unresolved pain, but I couldn't shake the belief that I had to do this to maintain some semblance of peace before our big day. Part of me was still clinging to the hope that this gesture would mend some of the brokenness between us.

Growing up, I watched my mom give my dad countless chances, no matter how many times he hurt her. That pattern of forgiveness became deeply ingrained in me, almost as if it was part of my DNA. It wasn't just something I learned, something I absorbed. I believed that holding on, even when it was painful, was a sign of strength. I watched my mom endure so much, and it left an imprint on my heart. I started to believe that perseverance in the face of pain was noble, and that never giving up on someone, especially family, was the ultimate act of love.

Deep down, I convinced myself that it was my responsibility to keep trying for reconciliation with my dad, no matter how strained the relationship had become. I found myself constantly seeking moments when we could connect. I invited him to concerts, dinners, and other events, hoping that maybe, just maybe, those small acts of reaching out could bridge the gap between us.

Each invitation felt like extending an olive branch, a way to say, "I'm still here, and I'm still trying." I convinced myself that by extending these invitations, I was honoring the lessons I had learned about forgiveness. I wanted to believe that holding on to relationships, even when they were difficult, was the right thing to do.

Dillon and I were married on September 6, 2015, in a beautiful country-chic ceremony that felt like a dream come true. The decor was filled with copper tones and sprigs of soft baby's breath, creating a warm, rustic atmosphere. As I walked down the aisle, my dad by my side, I felt a mixture of emotions.

Our vows were simple but profound: "I choose you every day," we said, looking deeply into each other's eyes. We shared a lighthearted moment as we both blew out the unity candle, laughter filling the air. The day was made even more special by the presence of more than 450 guests who joined us in celebrating our love and helped make it an unforgettable occasion.

I got to marry my best friend that day. It was the best decision I've ever made.

Dillon, I still choose you every day.

CHAPTER
ELEVEN
The Hardest Goodbye

Though Mom and Dad had separated after nine very hard years of marriage, she still chose to attend my wedding with him, holding on to a lingering hope for their relationship. She loved him deeply, even though their marriage had been strained for so long. Despite the separation, she clung to the belief that something could still be salvaged. My dad, always masterful at using his charm, casually mentioned after the wedding that maybe things wouldn't be so bad after the divorce.

"It'll be all right, Deanna," he said with an air of detachment. "We can still date, go to the movies, or whatever. Nothing will really change." His words seemed to mesmerize her, and she clung to them as if he were offering a lifeline. It was heartbreaking to witness how she continued to believe in his empty promises, as if she were under some kind of spell and unable to see the truth.

In the months following our wedding, the dynamics shifted even further. My dad pulled away emotionally, throwing himself into longer work hours and leaving me to grapple with the reality of having suffered from his emotional abuse. I found myself avoiding his calls, needing space to process everything that had been said and done when he threatened my life that day in the kitchen.

Meanwhile, I was navigating my new life with Dillon and trying to build a future with him. When I first married Dillon, I thought it was too good to be true, and I stayed fearful. Just because I was out of the atmosphere of the narcissistic abuse I'd been raised in did not mean I was free. My anxiety kept following me. I was trying to learn how to love Dillon and build our marriage, all while trying to make sense of the complexities surrounding my parents' relationship. It was a delicate balance, one I wasn't fully prepared for. But in the end, I knew I had to focus on my own happiness and the future I wanted to create. I was committed to my new life with my husband.

One day as I sorted through the mail, I came across a package from my dad. I slowly opened it, not sure what to think. Inside was a handwritten poem about how proud he was of me and how he loved his daughter so much. Out fell a shiny tube of expensive Chanel lipstick, plus my favorite perfume, Mademoiselle by Chanel. It was an early birthday gift. I thought this gesture was very thoughtful, but I was also skeptical. We hadn't talked in quite a while. I thanked him in a text message and continued on with my day.

However, my one text message caused him to send me a bunch right back. You know how they say when you give an inch, people will take a mile? His messages kept coming, and they were strange and disjointed. He kept mentioning a name I had never heard—*Clara*. I began to receive floods of messages from him, eventually hundreds of texts, talking about this mystery woman.

Are you and Clara hanging out?
Clara sure is a pretty friend you have.
When are you going to see Clara again?
I sure do miss Clara.

I bet Clara is having so much fun with you!

Clara is a beautiful girl. What are you two doing today?

What now? Who's Clara? I didn't know what was going on so I responded with something vague like, "Yeah, thanks, we are having a great time," even though I didn't know anyone named Clara!

His text messages were annoying and confusing. Each time I heard my dad's text alert sound, a jolt of anxiety shot through me. These texts persisted for months, each one more confusing than the last. I didn't want to provoke him, so I played along, masking my growing concern. It wasn't until a routine, ordinary moment in the car while applying my Chanel lipstick that everything became clear. As I put the tube away, I happened to turn it over and see the label attached on the bottom—*Clara*.

The realization hit me like a ton of bricks, and my heart raced as I had a sickening, stomach-drop feeling. The connection between his obsessive messages and the lipstick was horrifyingly clear. Without a second thought, I rolled down the window and threw the lipstick out of the car window, feeling disgusted by my dad's behavior. *I can't do this any longer*, I told myself. I needed the crazy mind games to stop. I just needed things to feel normal for once in my life.

As I look back on that moment, I was deeply troubled by how my dad seemed to be humanizing an object, projecting a bizarre fixation onto something as mundane as my lipstick. His mental state was increasingly frightening, and it felt like the person I had once known was no longer there. Each night, I tossed and turned, plagued by worries about his well-being. I prayed for him constantly, desperate for a glimpse of hope. I realized I was truly losing him. Even though this man had brought me so much pain and sadness, the core truth that he was my father kept me connected to him, feeling sorry for him, and concerned about him.

Yet I had been hurt by this man so many times, each wound piling onto the last, compounding the trauma. I was emotionally exhausted and completely drained. Forgiveness felt impossible, and I didn't want to give him any more of my energy. But I felt like I had to—he was still my dad. So I drew on a deep, unwavering strength to bury the pain and swallow the hurt as once again I tried my best to forgive and forget, even in the absence of an apology. I went to therapy in an attempt to figure out how to communicate with him more effectively. I refused to let bitterness take root in my heart. But after several counseling sessions, I knew I needed resolution.

Despite all my reservations, I found myself at a crossroads, unsure of where else to turn. In a moment of desperation, I threw a big Hail Mary and sent Dad a text, inviting him to a joint counseling session. To my surprise, he accepted eagerly, and a small flicker of hope ignited within me. Could this be the turning point I'd been waiting for? Could this finally be the opportunity to heal the years of pain and fractured trust? I promised myself that this would be his final chance—either we would work through our past, or I would have to let go completely. But I had to try, both for my own sake and for the sake of our relationship.

As I sat in the therapist's waiting room before he arrived, my heart raced with a mixture of fear and hope. I prayed with everything I had, asking for a genuine change of heart on my dad's part. I prayed that I would be strong enough to listen, understanding enough to allow room for growth, and wise enough to protect myself from further hurt. My mind was filled with questions: *Can Dad truly change? Will this moment finally be the breakthrough I've been longing for?* Over the years, my relationship with my dad had stayed calm as long as I didn't share my opinions, agreed with him on everything, and suppressed my emotions. But I just couldn't live that way anymore.

When my father walked through the door, I looked at him with a blend of anticipation and guardedness. I searched his eyes, hoping to see some sign of sincerity, and in that fleeting moment it seemed like maybe it was there. We sat down with the counselor, and for the next five hours we poured out our hearts, unearthing years of unresolved pain. My chest tightened with every word, but I held on to a thread of hope that this conversation could lead to healing.

To my astonishment and overwhelming relief, Dad apologized for everything. For the first time, he acknowledged the deep hurt he had caused throughout my life. There were no excuses, no attempts to shift blame or manipulate the situation. He took full responsibility for his actions. He owned up to everything—*everything*. It felt like a weight had been lifted from my shoulders as he spoke. In that moment, I could see he was truly making himself vulnerable, and for the first time, I allowed myself to believe that change could be possible.

We embraced tightly, and I felt tears streaming down my face as the years of pent-up emotions finally broke free. It was as if I had been holding my breath for a lifetime, and now I could finally exhale. My dad looked at me with softened eyes and told me I was beautiful. "I am so proud of you," he said. His words, so simple yet so powerful, touched a part of me that had been buried for far too long. It was the moment I had been waiting for. *He finally sees me—he truly sees me— for who I am and sees the pain I have carried for so long.*

In that counseling room, for the first time in years, I felt heard. He acknowledged my pain, my insecurities, and my hesitations about him. It was a moment of clarity and release, one that allowed me a glimmer of hope for the future. We both apologized, and in the aftermath of our long-awaited conversation, we made a pact: *We will work on rebuilding our relationship.*

It wasn't going to be easy. I knew it wasn't going to happen overnight, but it was a start. And for me, that was enough. And for the first time in a long time, I felt a calm settle inside me, a flicker of hope that maybe, just maybe, healing could happen.

After our session, we went out to dinner, though I drove separately. I was still feeling really proud of my dad. For the first time in a long while, we were able to speak to each other in a way we hadn't before. The conversation was lighthearted and filled with laughter as we reminisced about old times. There was no heavy tension, no undercurrent of unspoken pain—just two people enjoying each other's company. It might have been casual, but it was progress, which I considered to be an answer to prayer.

As I looked at him, I recognized his warm smile, something I hadn't seen in ages. It was a small but significant moment—*My dad is back*. The joy and relief that washed over me were indescribable. It felt like a weight had been lifted from my chest, like a storm had finally passed through. As I drove home that night, happy tears streamed down my face, my heart swelling with emotions I had long suppressed. I felt truly seen and understood by him, not as a child or an afterthought, but as a person he valued and respected. This reconnection, this glimpse of the father I had always longed for, gave me a sense of peace and acceptance I had been dreaming of my whole life.

The next morning, I woke up beyond excited. I believed in the possibility of a fresh start. The nightmare I'd been living with for so long seemed to be behind me. We had finally reached a place where communication could begin, where we could rebuild what had been broken. I felt hopeful, relieved, and ready to move forward.

I called him immediately after waking up, eager to express how much the previous day had meant to me. "Good morning, Daddio!" I said cheerfully. "I just wanted you to know how thankful I am that you went to counseling with me yesterday and paid for dinner. You didn't have to do that. You really do mean so much to me, and I'm so grateful we can start fresh. I'm looking forward to seeing you soon. I love you so much!"

Nothing could have prepared me for his response. Without any warning, he erupted into an explosion of anger that felt all too familiar. His voice—loud, venomous, and full of rage—punched through the calm. I was shocked by the sheer dishonesty and hatred in what he screamed over the phone that day. Not only did he deny ever going to counseling with me or taking me to dinner the night before, but he also insisted there was nothing wrong with him and accused me of being a delusional liar.

But it was the words he said at the end of the call that hurt the most:

"I don't love you. I never have. I don't want to know you. I don't care about you and your life. *Go to hell.*"

Then he hung up the phone. His words hit hard and deep, instantly cutting through the hope and peace I had begun to feel. I was stunned, completely blindsided. In that moment, everything that had seemed to shift the day before came crashing down. I felt utterly broken, shattered in a way I knew could never be pieced together.

I kept replaying everything in my head, trying to figure out how someone could change so fast. How could he go from being open to working things out to saying something so hurtful and shattering? I questioned everything. Was I wrong to believe things could change? Was he ever truly sincere? The confusion and heartache were overwhelming, and I couldn't make sense of the emotional whiplash I was experiencing. It was as though all the hope I had built up vanished in an instant, replaced by a sadness deeper than I had ever known. Was he suffering from a severe mental illness?

This was the final straw. I had promised myself I'd try one last time, and my inner child was screaming, begging me not to break that promise. Promises mean everything to me, and I wasn't about to let myself get pulled back into his dysfunction. Anyone can say they're sorry a million times, but without real repentance and genuine change, I knew I couldn't waste my time on him anymore. He was simply manipulating me.

I knew what I had to do, and this time I was determined to follow through. His reaction made it clear that no resolution was possible.

With shaking hands and tears streaming down my face, I sent him one final message: "Goodbye. You will never see me again or know my future children."

After I sent that text, I blocked his number, fully aware that this was a necessary step for my own well-being, although I hated to do it. It was as if every emotion I had bottled up inside poured out all at once—grief, regret, and a deep, aching pain. Yet in the midst of all the heartache, there was a sense of freedom, and despite the brokenness, I knew I was finally letting go of something that had held me captive for far too long.

This decision to cut ties wasn't just about cutting off a relationship; it was about acknowledging the painful truth that no matter how much I wished for a different outcome, some things were beyond my control. It was about accepting that I had done everything I could, exhausted all possible avenues, and now had to face the reality that preserving my own mental health and future happiness required a heartbreaking sacrifice.

As a little girl, I sat beside my mom many times as I watched her cry over the pain my dad caused her. Her heartache was undeniable, each tear a reminder of the love she so desperately wanted to hold on to even as it was slowly being torn apart. I would sit there, my small hand resting on hers, trying to offer comfort in the only way I knew how. I'd tell her, "Mama, you can't hug a knife." At the time, those words were just something I said to make her feel better, a simple statement that I thought could maybe, just maybe, take away some of her pain and sadness. I didn't fully understand the weight of those words then—how sharp the metaphor truly was, how much truth these few words held.

You *can't* hug a knife. It may seem like a simple image, but it's a powerful one. An unhealthy person is like a knife, and no matter how badly you want to hold them close, no matter how much you crave their love or approval, they will only wound you. At first, you tell yourself that with enough patience and love, they'll soften—that somehow you can fix them. But each time you reach out, that blade digs deeper. It doesn't care about your heart, your sacrifices, or your hopes. It only grips. It cuts into your spirit, your sense of self, until you're left bleeding inside, broken and bruised. The more you try to hold on, the more it destroys you.

> An unhealthy person is like a knife, and no matter how badly you want to hold them close, no matter how much you crave their love or approval, they will only wound you.

An unhealthy person will never give us the care or respect we need, leaving us feeling hollow, torn, and empty. We can't heal by holding on to something that only causes pain.

Sometimes the most loving thing we can do for ourselves is let go.

TWELVE

Lights, Cameras, and Contradictions

After spending more than twenty years silencing my voice and stuffing down my emotions just to keep peace with my dad, I was tired—mentally and emotionally drained. So when I joined *19 Kids and Counting*, I didn't want to keep pretending. I just wanted to show up as myself and be real.

And because I believed in the seemingly perfect world my uncle Jim Bob and my aunt Michelle had created for all my cousins, I thought they would care about my feelings. But as I shared earlier, when I was named "Crazy Cousin Amy" to add to the show's entertainment, I told Uncle Jim Bob how it made me feel. He laughed it off, telling me it wasn't a big deal. I was frustrated and upset that my uncle was essentially telling me that what I needed or wanted didn't matter. His dismissal of my very real concerns about being called "crazy" on a worldwide popular TV show made me feel like I had even less of a voice. My dad made sure I felt small and weak; my uncle's careless response made me feel even smaller and weaker.

I hated the "Crazy Cousin Amy" name because I detested the negative connotation it carried and felt like I was wearing a scarlet letter for absolutely no reason. But I decided to roll with it; after all, there was nothing I could do to change it. I had no power, no leverage, and no voice. In my opinion, Uncle Jim Bob made sure of that.

What people don't know is that *19 Kids and Counting* had been on the TLC cable network for a season and was starting to lose its initial spark. The network needed a boost in ratings, which meant trying something new. The production company first considered hiring a girl from California to live with the family to showcase the stark contrast in lifestyles. Instead, I became the contrast character they were looking for. As a family member who already was familiar with their rules and restrictions, it was easier to trust me since I was part of the family, and Uncle Jim Bob could control both the story line and me. Just like my grandmother, my uncle inherited a strong need for control. He was the unquestioned leader, the ultimate authority in deciding what his children could and could not do. Uncle Jim Bob often seemed to make up rules on the spot, and whenever something made him uncomfortable, his favorite response was a firm and unwavering no.

My uncle and I exchanged playful banter both on and off the screen for a very long time, and I looked up to him and trusted him. I believed at the time that he had the best interests of everyone at heart. I never doubted his love for me or his children. So I showed up as requested to take part in the filming frequently, especially at my cousins' house.

At first, I was having so much fun that I didn't think about whether I should get compensation for being a regular on the show because I had no concept of how people got paid to be on TV. I figured you had to be a huge star to earn anything. Then after six weeks of filming weekly, I was sent a lengthy contract by the network. I couldn't afford a lawyer to review it, so Grandma told me to ask my uncle to look at it for me. Since he already worked with the network, Grandma assured me he would advise me well (she thought my uncle hung the moon). Uncle Jim Bob read through it and encouraged me to sign. "It's a great opportunity for you," he said.

I trusted him and signed the contract without hesitation, though I hadn't read through it on my own. I didn't know that I was, in a sense, signing my life away.

Later on, I felt like an idiot for being so trusting. At the time, I didn't know I was agreeing to zero compensation, and that for years to come it would be mandatory for me to be at the network's beck and call whenever they needed me. While the show made our lives look fun and lighthearted, the work was real. We were filmed into the early morning hours, endured eight-hour interview days, had to wear the same clothes and keep our hair and makeup the same for days to ensure continuity, and could spend a couple of weeks filming to create a one-hour episode. Filming was so different from real life. There were moments that felt completely unnatural—like when we had to walk through the same door fifty times just because a baby was crying or someone sneezed at the wrong moment.

I also didn't know that my contract stated that *any* life-altering moment in my life could be filmed, including funerals, weddings, and childbirth. I would not only be filming without any compensation but also be unable to take a full-time job anywhere. So, then, how was I supposed to earn an income?

I can't believe I was encouraged to blindly sign the document. When I realized I had put myself in such a terrible position, I remember crying and shaking, sick to my stomach about the costly mistake I had just made. I was so naive and stupid to believe my uncle was looking out for me.

At that time, I didn't think my uncle had any ill intentions. Now I think maybe he did. He probably saw an opportunity to avoid paying me and to use my likeness without spending a single dime. My grandma was disappointed in her son's actions, so she did what she could for me. She would buy me clothes for the show, surprise me with extra groceries, and slip money into my wallet when I wasn't looking. She's the reason I started saving any money at all.

As I spent more time on set for the show, I started to notice details of the family dynamics I hadn't seen before. Uncle Jim Bob's control over the show and our lives became more apparent. He managed every aspect of the show's production, including our involvement. Our film crew, although they seemed like great people, answered to Jim Bob, and Jim Bob only. If I had a question, it was always quickly dismissed. I was constantly aware of my behavior and appearance, knowing that even the smallest misstep or any disapproval could result in being excluded from filming.

I cherished the quality time we spent together and genuinely wanted to be a part of the show, but I also understood there was a fine line between being carefree and crossing into sinful behavior. I tried to navigate that line, though to be honest, I wasn't always sure exactly where it was.

Uncle Jim Bob did let me know he appreciated the spice I brought to the show because some of his children were very shy and would hardly speak. I was known for being brave and adventurous, willing to jump on a huge hog, go skydiving, and sometimes bend the rules. I wasn't afraid to try new things or make a fool out of myself. And since I'd already been labeled "Crazy Cousin Amy," I figured I had two options: I could either hate my new nickname or embrace it. So I decided that instead of viewing that label as a negative, I would try to see it as an endearing title describing a happy-go-lucky character who would do anything for a laugh.

Sure, I'll feed bread from my mouth to the giraffe.
Sure, I'll get all muddy looking for diamonds.

Sure, I'll try to knit baby booties, burn a dessert, and get dunked in a dunk tank.

I didn't take myself too seriously and wasn't trying to get more attention than others. But I was always up for some fun, and the show highlighted that side of me. I became the go-to person for any wild or wacky activity that my uncle or the producers dreamed up. This dynamic created a balance on the show that Uncle Jim Bob understood was necessary and could be addictive to the audience.

My cousins, especially the shier ones, often needed a bit of encouragement to come out of their shells, and I provided that spark. My antics and boldness gave them the space to participate in their own way, knowing I was there to fall back on to make things more entertaining if needed. My uncle is smart and creative, and even though he didn't allow his family to watch TV or movies, he had a knack for knowing how to boost the ratings.

My willingness to do just about anything backfired on me in an episode called "First Grandson Turns 1." When I arrived for filming at the big house around 8:00 a.m., the producer took me aside and said, "Amy, today you are going to create a Noah's ark birthday cake."

What! I don't have the first clue how to do that. Where do I buy all the animals?

I soon found out how and where, spending the entire day driving all over the place to purchase ingredients and decorations to fulfill my assignment—to bake a huge cake that could feed more than sixty people. The film crew followed me everywhere as I looked for toy animals. I was in such a hurry that I used my card to pay for everything, and it wasn't cheap. I bought cake mix, icing, pans, and pairs upon pairs of animals from a specialty store. It took a lot of dollars, effort, and gas.

This episode sticks out in my mind because it was the first time the question came up: *Where does all the money from the show go?*

After that long day, I went to Uncle Jim Bob and kindly asked him if I could be reimbursed for the items I bought. After all, I had no use for the animals. The network would use them for the television show. Plus, it was the *first* time I had asked for any compensation. And the reality was, I didn't have any extra money to spare.

"Now, Amy, this is a ministry," my uncle said. "You chose to do this special project, and you should be grateful for the opportunity." Jim Bob often spoke about having a "ministry mindset," emphasizing how we had a unique opportunity to reach people who were lost. He framed it as a calling, as a responsibility to use our platform for something bigger than ourselves. I realized quickly that Uncle Jim Bob didn't care that I had been asked to bake the cake or that I would have to use my own money and gas.

I was so mentally exhausted from the whole baking debacle, I decided not to stay for the party, and so I didn't get a bite of the cake I made. As I was walking out to my car, completely depleted and worried about how much money I spent, a producer walked over to me and shook my hand. Then he slipped me $600. "I wish I could pay you more than this, but that's all the extra I have," he said.

It felt like a drug deal—very hush-hush, completed out of sight of the others. I remember thinking, *If the producer just handed me $600 in cash, how much is my time on the show actually worth?*

I left feeling grateful for the money but really distraught, because I felt misunderstood and undervalued. I've struggled with feeling small and worthless since I was a young child, always made to believe I didn't amount to much and had nothing to offer. Now I was on a show where I was again being manipulated to question my worth. It was clear that my uncle didn't care about my financial struggles. I had no idea at the time that he was denying me an income while he was raking in tens of thousands of dollars per episode.[1]

When I first started working as a nanny before the show aired,

I opened a savings account with just $100. I continued to save most of my earnings while nannying five days a week. I worked through holidays and sometimes put in twelve-hour days or more. I tried to maintain a social life and have some fun, but I was frugal. I *had* to be.

Now here I was, a cast member on a hugely successful show, and I had even more expenses. I had to buy my own makeup and hair products for the show, and I would regularly shop at Goodwill to find something "new" to wear. And my car always had to be filled with gas because the producers had me running all over the county for different episodes.

It was a constant hustle and juggling act. I started to feel like I was being taken advantage of. I was doing everything I could to keep up with the demands of filming while still nannying for seven different well-to-do families so I'd have some income. In addition to being a fun nanny to so many kiddos, I was also trying to have a social life and manage the chaotic circumstances with my parents. It was exhausting.

Even so, I was expected to smile on cue for the cameras, watch what I said, try to blend in, not draw too much attention to myself, have fun, be spontaneous, laugh on cue, and go on adventures, all while my bank account was being drained. Rumors started to circle online that I was using my family for fame, while at the same time my dad was having psychotic episodes. I started to feel like a puppet on strings. I was already known for being "crazy," and under all the pressure, I seriously felt like I was spiraling out of control.

I continued to work hard, filming season after season of *19 Kids and Counting*—more than eighty episodes—without pay, while my uncle was raking in millions, as I eventually came to find out.

If he was grateful for my contributions, he certainly didn't show it. Instead, it felt like the Institute in Basic Life Principles way of life was invading my space. My uncle didn't often approve of my outfits, so I always kept extra clothes in my car just in case I needed to change.

He told me I was too loud and had to blend in during certain scenes, and that my personality was "too much to handle." He told me that I needed to remember that it wasn't my show, and that it never would be. (I usually replied with some version of "I'm not editing the episodes.")

He warned me that I'd attract the wrong kind of man if I didn't behave, and offered to help find me a husband. "I'm a great match-maker, and I can find you a suitable man to help calm you down," he said. He thought big jewelry would draw too much negative attention and make me look like a harlot, so I wasn't allowed to wear my jewelry. And I certainly wasn't permitted to wear ball caps because those were only for boys.

I once brought friends over to my uncle's house, including a close friend who was Black. Uncle Jim Bob later took me into his office and explained that it was okay to be friends with this man, but nothing more. I felt that it was because of the color of his skin. I couldn't believe the words that were coming out of my uncle's mouth. Even so, I nodded quietly and kept my mouth shut. But what I thought was, *Uncle Jim Bob, let's get something straight. Whoever I decide to date is none of your business, and if you ask me, God looks at the heart of a person, and that's what matters!*

I was always being called to his office like a rebellious student being sent to the principal's office for no reason.

I also got the feeling that if Uncle Jim Bob thought I was getting too much camera time, I wouldn't be invited to attend some of the extra-fun events. And it seemed like every time I made a request to participate in a certain activity or go to a place I was excited about, he would deny me. I had only a few specific requests—learning to do fencing, for example—during the entire time we filmed. And yet each one was denied.

One of the trips I was most excited about was hanging out in the Great Smoky Mountains and meeting Dolly Parton. *Hello, who doesn't want to meet Dolly?* But my grandma, my mom, and I weren't invited to join in on that trip. My uncle bluntly told us, "If you want to go, find your own way."

So we did!

We arrived in time to wait in a large room at Dollywood for Dolly to arrive. I tried hard to blend in with my cousins so my uncle would be pleased, but Dolly gave me a hug and said, "I know exactly who you are. You are feisty like me!" I just loved that compliment coming from such a huge icon. She had no idea how much I needed that validation. Thank you, Dolly!

I was completely banned from joining whenever Bill Gothard of IBLP visited the Duggar home. His visits seemed like covert missions I could never be informed of. I thought it was strange because the big house seemed to have an open-door policy. Media coverage was allowed, other IBLP families visited, and sometimes it seemed as busy as an airport or train station, with people coming and going all the time. Surely it was sometimes difficult to keep track of all your kids and make sure they were safe, yet that wasn't what they seemed worried about. But having me there at the same time as Bill Gothard? That seemed to make them quake in their boots.

I would have liked to meet him. As the founder of IBLP, Bill Gothard is an extremely significant character for my family. But despite my many questions, I never got the chance to ask him about his beliefs. I wanted to understand so much more about the principles that shaped my family's way of life. Yet, big shocker, I was never given the opportunity.

People always ask me, "How was your relationship with your cousins when you weren't filming?" Well, here's the honest truth: I felt like I was constantly kept at arm's length. It was as if my cousins cared for me, but an invisible barrier prevented them from truly letting me in. It wasn't just emotional distance; it was like they weren't *allowed* to get close to me. It was the strangest thing. My mom and I would run into them in public, and instead of acting like we were family, they would treat us as if we were just random fans of the show. They'd say a polite hello, but it was the kind of greeting you give someone you barely know. I grew up with these people and had known them my whole life. I wondered how we had gone from being family to being strangers in a crowd. I could only guess it was the way Uncle Jim Bob was continuing to control the narrative.

That treatment was in stark contrast to the person I wanted to be— authentic and loyal, someone who seeks the good in others. I didn't know it then, but I was already becoming a holy disruptor, someone who could see what true loyalty and authenticity should be and offered that to others, no matter how I was being treated.

CHAPTER
THIRTEEN

Happily Brainwashed

Being kept at arm's length by my uncle and his family had a profound impact on me. Even though they were kind to me, they always made me feel like an outsider. While my cousins would politely talk to me, I never really felt like I knew any of them personally except for Josh. We never discussed our feelings or private struggles, and we certainly never talked about our relationship with God.

Eventually I realized my cousins lived in a closed system. We weren't allowed to have open conversations because I wasn't part of the Institute in Basic Life Principles, and they knew I was off-limits. IBLP teaches that one should only be close to those who share the same principles, which inevitably created a wall between us. I felt the distance not so much because I was blocked from engaging in certain activities; instead, it resulted from the constant messaging that I wasn't truly part of the family: "We love Amy, but . . ." There was always some kind of stipulation. One minute, my uncle would invite me to help with whatever they needed on camera, and the next, he'd change his mind and not want me around because he thought I was too disruptive.

One day, I returned home feeling depressed and sad about how I was being treated and the lack of compensation for my work. My mom hated to see me struggle. She could see the hurt and confusion in my eyes every time we visited them. So she called her brother in a rage and said, "I'm tired of my daughter receiving crumbs at the king's table." Later that day, my uncle sent one of his boys over with $800 for me.

That money was helpful because I continued to face significant financial challenges, which made it even harder to witness the abundance my uncle had. Their house often felt more like a bustling hotel than a family home. It reminded me of the chaotic opening scene from the movie *Home Alone*. There was always a flurry of activity, girls headed off on shopping sprees, new computers lining the countertops, and used cars filling the driveway as if they were car collectors. Real estate purchases were happening left and right. My uncle and his family lived in a world where money seemed to flow effortlessly. I wasn't consumed by jealousy. Rather, it was more a sense of astonishment. Their wealth was in stark contrast to my tight budget. It was difficult not to feel disheartened.

I also found myself constantly questioning why my involvement on the show seemed to hold no weight in my uncle's eyes. No matter how hard I worked or how much I contributed, it felt as though it all went unnoticed. My personality was simply different from the rest of my family. I often felt like I had to tone myself down, second-guessing whether my sense of humor was appropriate or if my outfit was acceptable since I didn't always wear skirts and dresses. Instead of feeling embraced for who I was, I was often met with aloofness, not just from my uncle and aunt, but from my cousins as well.

Much of the rejection I experienced stemmed from rigid expectations, where following rules was more important than offering love and understanding. It felt like my faith was judged by how I dressed, how softly I spoke, or whether I knew the words to every hymn. If my beliefs didn't perfectly match theirs, I was left feeling locked out and disconnected. I was already battling feelings of unworthiness because of my father, and now I was facing the same struggle in my extended family. Some days, I'd leave their house and cry the entire way home, questioning why I never seemed to belong.

Despite all the turmoil, they were my family, and I genuinely cared about them. I didn't want to cause problems; I just wanted to be part of their lives, to be loved and treated fairly. I longed for acceptance and belonging, but in the Duggar family, standing out wasn't something to be proud of. The constant scrutiny and judgment made me want to blend in more than anything else. Sure, they knew my favorite color, my love for sweets, and my fear of clowns, but the deep stuff—the heart-to-heart talks, the moments of vulnerability, the things that shaped who I am—they knew nothing about. It left me with a strange and hollow feeling, being very aware that they didn't really know the real me and that I had never had the chance to truly know them.

What I did know was that my cousins were pranksters, always looking for an opportunity to have a little fun at my expense. Sometimes when I came over to the house, they snuck around and grabbed my keys from the counter, unlocked my car, started the engine, and changed all my radio presets to AM gospel channels. A note would be taped to my steering wheel that read, "Music was designed to promote joy in the heart of man." Now, I wasn't a heavy, hard rock and roller. I loved '80s music, country hits like "Goodbye Earl," and the occasional rap song. For the most part, I was cautious about what I listened to, but they felt the need to preach at me whenever they got the chance.

Sometimes driving home after a long day of filming, I'd be about ten minutes down the road and I'd hear giggling. Some of the younger boys would be stowed away in my trunk. Their pranks were usually harmless and fun. But one time they took it a bit too far, filling my car with confetti and glitter—tons of glitter left over from a birthday party sprinkled on my cloth upholstery! While I was a little overwhelmed by the mess, I was happy that they were comfortable enough to joke around with me.

The boys were full of personality, cracking jokes and coming up with the most creative ideas. With them I could let loose and have fun. But most of the girls were reserved, quiet, and hesitant to make their presence felt. When I was with them, I sometimes felt like I wasn't proper enough to fit in. I wondered if I came across as too casual or rough around the edges because I didn't speak with the soft, sweet, princess-like tone so many IBLP wives have perfected. When I was in my teens, I asked my mom, "Since I don't talk like that, do I sound like a man?"

What stood out the most, though, was that I had never once heard any of my cousins get upset, raise their voice, or show any kind of attitude. Not my aunt, not my uncle—no one. It was as though negative emotions didn't exist in their world, or at least weren't allowed to be seen.

Being at my cousins' house felt stifling at times, like laughter had exceeded its expiration date. Everyone could be so serious. I vividly remember having a surprising conversation one day with a younger cousin. He turned to me with genuine curiosity and asked, "Amy, what does the word *worship* mean to you? How do you worship?"

I answered honestly, "To me, it means honoring God daily with my life and making sure he's at the center. But honestly, that can be really hard sometimes."

He shook his head, unsatisfied with my response. "No, Amy, worship isn't about that. Worship is you on your hands and knees, reading Scripture for hours," he insisted. "That's why we have a prayer closet. Maybe you'd make different life choices if you really worshiped God."

My young cousin's suggestion that I should turn my clothing closet into a prayer space, complete with a little desk and a Bible, left me both puzzled and amused. I wanted to tell him that while there's nothing wrong with having a designated space for prayer, I couldn't help but wonder, with a prayer regimen like that, *Do you ever get bored?*

Also, who has time to pray *for hours*? I hoped my cousins took breaks, and seriously, do they have a pillow or at least some kind of cushion for their knees?

It felt like my cousins were trapped in an outdated mindset. We aren't under the laws of the Old Testament anymore. God wants to be in our hearts, our daily activities, and our demeanor and conduct—he wants more than pretty words spoken in a prayer closet. Yet instead of engaging in a deeper discussion, I just smiled softly at my young cousin and left the conversation thinking, *What the heck are they teaching these kids?*

The conversation was a stark reminder of the rigid interpretations of faith that were being handed down, making life as a believer feel more like a checklist of behaviors rather than a genuine relationship with God. I couldn't shake the feeling that worship should be a vibrant part of life, woven into everyday moments and not confined to a single space or rigid practice. I had so many conversations like that one with my cousins, but after a while I tuned them out. They were constantly preaching at me, and I just couldn't engage them anymore.

At least once while in their teens, each of my boy cousins was sent to a camp called International ALERT Academy, a controversial Christian program funded by Bill Gothard. The camp operates as paramilitary training. The teens are taught survival skills boot camp–style, where they practice hard work and learn what it takes to be a godly man. Upon arrival, they are not allowed to speak for days and are tested to the extreme physically, mentally, and emotionally. Participants are required to study and memorize Scripture word for word and undergo physical training in the form of military drills that are rigorous and exhausting. Throughout the day, participants experience constant supervision, limited personal time, restricted communication with the outside world, and emphasis on conformity to Bill Gothard's interpretation of biblical principles and authority structures.

Sometimes I felt like my cousins lived in a completely different world than mine. When my aunt and uncle were first married, they hosted a large bonfire and invited other IBLP families to bring Disney items to toss into the fire because Disney promoted magic and fairy tales. Yet in my house, I would dress up as a little girl and pretend to be Belle from *Beauty and the Beast* and act like a mermaid in the bathtub—the kind of imaginative play that was forbidden in their home. My cousins knew nothing about the latest movies, styles, trends, or magazines. They didn't recognize celebrities, watch popular TV shows, go to concerts, or hang out at the local mall. Their entertainment was limited to listening to Bible stories on the AM radio. My cousins had no way of knowing about current events or any local happenings in our town. I remember my mom once called my uncle to let him know about a tornado warning.

Children's books were very limited. If the book had pictures that showed a person's shoulder or kneecap, the cousins would grab a permanent black marker and color over that part of the picture. I'm not sure when the black marker thing got started, but it happened all the time. It was like the kids were afraid because they didn't want to disappoint their parents.

They'd also color over magazine pictures and family pictures. I know for a fact that my wedding picture was colored in. All of my cousins' wedding dresses were beautiful and modest, but honestly, I was happy that mine stood out. My dress was strapless, showing some cleavage and my clavicle. I know they marked up my photo with black ink to add coverage. If they didn't like a photo in which someone was wearing clothing that wasn't up to their standards, they'd color it in without hesitation.

If my cousins came over to our house for any special reason, like a birthday or to watch their own reality show, we had to hold a sheet over the television during the commercials. I remember the time we got to chatting, which led to a failure to cover the television quickly enough. As a result, my cousins saw a glimpse of a body wash commercial. My younger girl cousins began to cry because of what they had seen. My uncle made a speech about why it's important to shield one's eyes, and that they didn't have a television in their home to avoid any chance they'd see something my uncle and aunt deemed inappropriate.

Beach vacations were highly frowned upon. If my cousins visited the ocean, they would go at night. The later they went to the beach, the less chance they'd see nakedness, and by *nakedness*, I mean girls in bikinis and guys without shirts. The Duggar kids couldn't wear shorts either. Even in the heat of summer, the boys had to walk around in either long khaki pants or jeans, sweating profusely. They looked miserable. I can't imagine how the boys felt to have to wear jeans to an amusement park in 100-plus degree heat.

Modest bathing suits, like those worn by ultraconservatives, were not allowed at all. One-piece swimming suits were considered immodest. Instead, they had to wear jumpsuit-style scuba gear, which often included a skirt to ensure that their figure wasn't visible.

They couldn't wear big pieces of jewelry or pierce their ears. Anyone who had pierced ears was considered to be in the bondage of the devil. However, clip-on earrings were acceptable. In an attempt to bring some sense of normalcy to the girls' world, I brought them some stick-on earrings. I also taught the girls the basics of cheerleading on the trampoline. I told them stories that were actually the story lines of movies, shared clean jokes they had never heard, and brought them special treats they had never had. I tried my best to be a part of their world, but I always felt I had to tiptoe around the rules. I wanted to introduce them to things I thought might help them feel more connected to other people and allow them to experience the culture. But I was careful not to do anything that might be considered wrong or harmful. They seemed to love my gifts and stories.

As they got older, the girls weren't allowed to get a job or dream of a career if it involved college. This restriction was strongly enforced by IBLP, which taught that college is the place to go if you want to be separated from the Lord. Instead, mothers are expected to teach their daughters domestic skills such as cooking, cleaning, and child-rearing. Girls are groomed for early marriage and motherhood, with no emphasis on career aspirations or higher education outside of homemaking. Oddly, my uncle encouraged my girl cousins to write personal letters to men in prison because he saw it as a part of their ministry to reach the lost.

Boys were encouraged to step into the political arena, which was romanticized as a platform for enacting change, upholding their principles, and protecting the "right" way of life. The thought of a Duggar son holding a position of power and making decisions that could shape our community and beyond would be recognized as a high achievement. (The very highest achievement, however, was being called into ministry.) My uncle always told us who to vote for, and during election season, we were texted a list of the candidates so we would know whose name to circle on the ballot. *Heaven forbid we might actually think for ourselves!*

My cousins were always well-mannered and flawlessly trained to help around the house. Domestic training began at a young age in the Duggar household. Girls as young as seven years old were expected to take on significant responsibilities inside the home, often acting as second mothers to their younger siblings. Their days were filled with tasks that would prepare them for their future roles as wives and mothers, reinforcing the belief that their primary purpose in life was to support their husbands and raise children. My girl cousins couldn't paint their nails a dark or moody color, and the color black was not only off-limits but considered sinful. Anything black represented the dark side, because Jesus, who is light, would never approve of the color black. Darker makeup shades like mauve and brown, and even makeup with shimmer, were frowned on, and creativity in the way you presented yourself was not allowed. The girls had to maintain a natural appearance. The rules were the rules, set in stone, and no one questioned why. If any of them felt an urge to be rebellious, they never showed it.

Like little minions at times, the kids had a ton of chores and adhered to a strict buddy system in which the older children were assigned to take care of the younger ones. If you were an older sibling, you might have one or even two little buddies to look after. This entailed being responsible for their meals, changing diapers, getting them dressed, and helping with their schooling. The girls would also assist with the younger girls and boys at bath time. It was so much responsibility to have at such a young age.

My mom was a single mother, and while she did her best, she couldn't provide the same level of structure as in my uncle's house—not even close. When I was quite young, Uncle Jim Bob once told my mom that I was unruly. You wouldn't find me sitting quietly in a chair; I was daring and would climb to the highest limb in the tree. Since I was more of a tomboy, my uncle expressed concern and offered to help raise me. He didn't like that I wore jeans and thought I needed more examples of godliness in my life. He was worried about how I would grow up and wanted me to learn the ways of IBLP.

I sometimes went with my uncle and aunt to IBLP conferences, including one memorable experience when I was in elementary school. All of the kids sat in a big room while learning Bible verses and "The Crayon Box Song," which I can still recite: "Wooah, red is the color of the blood that Jesus shed, brown is for the crown of thorns they placed upon his head. Wooah, blue is for the royalty which in him did dwell, yellow's for the Christian too afraid to tell."[2]

After the lesson, we'd break up into small groups to learn definitions of big religious words, Bible verses, and songs. It was a four-hour-long ordeal, and I remember wondering why there was no break time or snack time. In order to leave the room and go home, we had to memorize and recite Scripture. I remember feeling panicked because I was one of the last ones in the room, struggling with one of the long verses. I didn't like feeling trapped and controlled, and I was terrified to have my release depend on how successful I was with a Bible verse. I couldn't understand why I had to memorize a Scripture verse word for word in order to be set free.

FOURTEEN

Drowning in a Sea of Expectations

When I was fourteen, I went to a traditional summer church camp. The week at camp was great, but I looked forward to getting back to my own bedroom. It was the coolest! I made it completely my own space, an oasis in my turbulent life. A bright purple satin comforter with pink and purple polka dots covered my bed; a lava lamp sat on the bedside table, with colorful blobs that rose and fell; and my collection of Lip Smackers adorned the vanity. Stacks of my favorite magazines, Lisa Frank sticker books, glow-in-the-dark stars on the walls, faux-fur picture frames, a spinning disco light, and inflatable furniture completed the setup.

So imagine my horror when I opened the door to my room to find all of my Jonathan Taylor Thomas and Spice Girls posters torn up and strewn around the carpet. My CDs of NSYNC, Brandy, Britney Spears, 98 Degrees, Backstreet Boys, Hanson, Faith Hill, and Shania Twain were all broken into pieces. My CD tower was empty, my diary opened, and my magazines shredded.

I was as hot as a firecracker! Apparently, some of my cousins had come over to visit my grandma and had quietly slipped into my room. Do I think they did it out of hatred? No. I knew they were trained to believe that destroying someone else's property was okay as long as they were destroying items that didn't honor the Lord. My cousins were taught to be good Christian soldiers—nothing else mattered, certainly not my feelings. They would tell you they were simply doing God's work.

As we got older and entered high school, I had a harder and harder time finding common ground with my cousins. They weren't allowed to have a crush, and their lives were missing the typical high school experiences—pressure, classes, and social dynamics—I was familiar with. They didn't know what Abercrombie was; they couldn't go to dances or listen to any music on FM radio stations; and the concept of a boyfriend or girlfriend was completely foreign to them. Their first kiss was reserved for their wedding day. I went to a few parties and had my first boyfriend when I was seventeen. But I couldn't talk to them about any of that because they couldn't relate and would only tell me how wrong it was to do what I was doing.

In a way, I envied their protected innocence. My first love wrecked me and broke my heart, an experience they would never have. Throughout my teens and twenties, I brought six guys over to the big house to meet my cousins, but every time a relationship ended, instead of simply acknowledging the breakup, my uncle would call me into his office and start lecturing me. He'd tell me it wasn't just a breakup; it was a mini divorce. "Amy, you are setting yourself up for a real divorce someday," he told me.

Dating was wrong in their eyes—a surefire way to end up divorced and alone. My uncle implied that dating multiple people was improper and that I was wasting time, as if there was only one right way to approach relationships. But it wasn't a waste of time. I was getting to know different personalities, figuring out what I truly needed in my life, and seeing who complemented my lifestyle. I wasn't interested in rushing into anything serious. Whether or not it lasted, each boyfriend taught me more about what I wanted and could offer in a partnership.

But in Uncle Jim Bob's mind, divorce was a sin, no matter the cause, even if it resulted from something as awful as abuse. Divorce simply could not be an option. If you were to get a divorce and remarry while still adhering to IBLP's rules, they believed God would not bless the new marriage, and so everyone treated you differently. So imagine the disgust on the faces of our extended family members when my parents broke ties and divorced.

I was always told, "God hates divorce," and for a while I believed IBLP had the correct view. But I see it differently now. Yes, marriage is something God has ordained. But if someone betrays our trust through something like infidelity or any type of abuse, I believe that the unfaithfulness or torment grieves God even more. Nobody deserves darkness behind closed doors.

After my parents' divorce, my aunt and uncle and cousins pretended like it didn't happen. Later on, my uncle called my mom and said, "Deanna, you need to stay single." Which is absurd—if anyone deserves a loving, healthy partnership, it's my mom. She doesn't deserve to be lonely for the rest of her life. She's a survivor, someone who has been through more than most people could imagine, yet she still carries herself with strength and grace. She deserves to have someone who cherishes her, someone who sees her true worth.

I loved my cousins and tried to respect the rules, but let's be honest, there were a lot of them. Each rule seemed to come with its own rationale, and I often felt overwhelmed trying to keep track of every single one. Courtship alone had a whole list of rules to follow. In the Duggar family, each courting couple had a chaperone who would sit between them on dates, listen in on their phone calls, and monitor their text messages. The chaperone's job was to give a report to my uncle on how everything went. This role was essential in keeping the couple accountable and ensuring they avoided any sexual temptation or even something as innocent as holding hands until they were given permission.

Can you imagine going on dates with the person you're engaged to but never having a moment alone? How could you truly be yourself or let down your guard when someone was always there, watching and listening? The chaperone's presence was a constant reminder of the family's strict rules and expectations. Every conversation, every gesture, every glance had to be carefully evaluated and judged to be appropriate. There was no room for spontaneous affection or private moments to connect on a deep level. The family's approach to relationships felt more like a transaction than a genuine connection. The constant oversight made it difficult to build an intimate bond and added an extra layer of stress to an already intense new stage of life.

I've always had to balance the challenge of steering away from the IBLP lifestyle while still craving approval from my family. It wasn't easy, trying to stay true to myself while also feeling pressure to meet their unrealistic expectations. Court one guy and not even kiss him until the wedding day? No thank you. Anyone can pretend to be perfect for a few months, especially when a chaperone is monitoring their every move and word. I didn't want a man who was just another rule follower or a vanilla cupcake. I wanted something different—a partner who was authentic, who could share his true self with me without the pretense and rigidity imposed by my family's beliefs. I craved a deeper and more meaningful connection with someone who wasn't afraid to break the mold, who could challenge me and grow with me. Modesty standards, courtship protocols—it was all so stifling. Maybe that's why I became more carefree. After a lifetime of rules being forced on me, many of which never made sense, I'd had enough.

I felt like I was drowning in a sea of expectations, unable to be myself. The rules were like chains, binding me to a life that wasn't mine. I didn't want to live in a world where my worth was measured by how well I adhered to those ridiculous standards. Everything was filtered through a narrow lens of what was considered acceptable by the Basic Life Principles.

Even now, I find myself questioning the logic behind many of the rules. They were presented as absolutes, but to me they often seemed inconsistent and contradicting. For example, we were taught to value honesty and integrity, yet we had to present a curated version of ourselves to the world, hiding anything that didn't fit the prescribed image. We were told to love unconditionally, yet the actual love offered was conditional—contingent on strict obedience to a specific set of beliefs. Everyone has bad days—we're human beings who have emotions, thoughts, and feelings. But none of my cousins could ever just be real. If they had a bad day, they knew how to hide it well. And questioning IBLP or any of the rules wasn't allowed. I learned early on that if I did, I'd only be invited to the house when Uncle Jim Bob was home to keep an eye on me. I learned to toe the line.

In an effort to prove I wasn't wild or rebellious, I even stopped wearing makeup and started dressing in long skirts and dresses, seeking to conform to their expectations. I thought that by changing my appearance, I might finally earn their acceptance and be seen as a godly person. But no matter how much I tried to fit in, I could never measure up to their standards.

One day, I decided to do a little experiment to see if they would treat me differently based on what I wore. For the next few months, I alternated outfits—one day, jeans with my hair up and heavy makeup on my eyes; the next day, a long maxi skirt or modest dress and light, natural makeup. The results were astounding. When I dressed in a more "worldly" style, the girls hardly spoke to me. They weren't rude, but I think it must have been hard for them to connect with me, since heavy makeup was considered ungodly and wearing jeans was viewed as a sin. The boys either avoided me altogether or felt compelled to save my soul. When I wore an outfit they approved of, the girls gathered around me on the couch, and the boys sat with me during lunch. I'd hear compliments like, "Skirts are so flattering on you," and "Wow, you look so pretty today." While I agree that skirts and dresses can be feminine and lovely, there's something to be said for the freedom to wear what I like. Still, despite being misunderstood, I did share a lot of fun and laughter with them.

While my cousins lived under the IBLP umbrella, we were also a family with a hit reality show. As ratings climbed, the perks got crazy! People reached out to me constantly on social media, wanting to send me jewelry, handbags, clothing, hair products, vitamins, and supplements. I was offered front-row tickets to events, hotel reservations, and almost anything else you could think of.

This kind of pampering created a distorted view of reality. When we were filming all day on the road, someone else handled all of the logistics, from paying for food to organizing activities and checking us in at airports and hotels. I didn't have to pay for my cell phone, and my insurance and passport costs were covered. We had the best seats for every event, never had to wait in lines at amusement parks, and ate in the best restaurants. The favors were endless, and wherever we went, we were always given VIP treatment and the grand tour.

It was great to have production cover our expenses for anything related to the show, because I never received compensation and couldn't afford to pay for those kinds of favors. After filming for long stretches where everything was paid for, it felt strange to suddenly be back in the real world where I had to pay for entertainment or food when I went out with friends. It was like being tossed from one world into another. I remember a time when I accidentally walked out of a restaurant without paying. The host had to flag me down in the parking lot. I felt terrible about it and quickly paid for my meal.

We were also becoming more recognizable in public. It seemed that everywhere we went people spotted us, and all of us were getting used to the popularity. I remember walking into a store with my aunt and a few cousins, only to see a line start to form with people who wanted to talk to us. Everywhere we went, people hugged us like we were long-lost friends. It was surreal. These strangers seemed to know everything about us.

While I tried my best to stay grounded, it became increasingly difficult to connect with others who led normal lives. My close friendships were tested, and I missed countless girls nights and birthday parties. My friends couldn't relate to the pressures I faced, and I struggled to be there for them in the way I wanted. The judgment and jealousy from those around me added to the strain. I didn't have to work hard to get the perks offered to me, and as a result, I lost sight of what real life was like and what hard work truly meant. I later realized how long it typically takes to earn the things that were simply given to me.

Along with the privilege of a higher status came the added pressure to excel and maintain the high standards set by my family, because they were the ones who provided these advantages. I constantly felt the weight of expectations resting on my shoulders, making me feel like I had to perform at all times. I couldn't afford to have a bad day. There was no room for taking it easy, even if I had cramps or a headache. Taking a day off was not an option. I was expected to be on set, ready to fulfill my role, because the show must go on—and the show needed Crazy Cousin Amy.

CHAPTER
FIFTEEN

"Famy"

We received mountains of mail throughout the year and especially at Christmastime, including countless crocheted gifts and heartfelt letters from adoring fans. Gift cards for restaurants and Amazon arrived with large balances. The media built us up to such an extent that I even found myself on the cover of *People* magazine. They called me after my wedding because they wanted to do a cover story, and I specifically told them, "I think you have the wrong family member." Despite all this, I never really considered myself famous; I was just the cousin to a famous family.

I had years and years of pampering, and although I'm grateful for the opportunities, it messed with my head. I really had to check myself because even the smallest taste of popularity can make me egotistical. I know that even though I tried to keep my ego in check, I failed at times. My mom called it "fame brain."

Reflecting back, I realize how surreal it was. It wasn't just about the material perks. The everyday experiences of others—simple tasks like checking in at the airport, renting a car, or handling any sort of minor inconvenience—were alien to me for a long time. Even my passport was expedited and ready to pick up the same day because I was flying out of the country on a whim. Though I was provided for, spoiled even, I still had to work as a nanny to earn an income.

I wasn't prepared for the moment I was put on a worldwide stage and how the floodgates would open to the harshest criticism imaginable. The pressures of social media transformed my life in unexpected ways. From random encounters in the supermarket in which people felt compelled to pray for my salvation to a surging number of Instagram followers, it all happened so fast. I received thousands of messages, and the swell in popularity brought with it an overwhelming wave of unsolicited opinions and relentless scrutiny.

People are quick to judge based on what they see on a screen, usually without knowing the full story. Trolls on social media will say anything behind the safety of their device. The problem with this behavior is that it dehumanizes the person on the receiving end. How many times can you be told, "You're so crazy," before you start to believe it? Bullies failed to realize that I am a real person, with feelings and experiences, who has a life outside of what they saw on their TV screen. Maybe they did realize it, and they just didn't care. All I know is that I've never pretended to be perfect, yet I was constantly judged as if I had claimed to be.

The nastiness of the comments got under my skin. Behind every screen is a human being who feels pain, just like everyone else. The internet makes it easy for people to lash out without pausing to consider the impact of their words. Reading hateful and hurtful messages day after day will take a serious toll on a person's mental health. They start to question their self-worth and doubt their abilities.

When I first started reading the vicious comments from viewers, I cried for days. With the weight of my dad's harsh words already heavy on my heart, I felt vulnerable and insecure. When media outlets and internet trolls began tearing me down and having a field day at my expense, I felt even smaller, crushing any sense of self-worth I had left. The feeling of being exposed and ridiculed, both by those closest to me and by strangers online, made me question everything about myself. Those questions haunted me for years. *Was I a mistake? Why am I even part of this family? What is wrong with me?*

I didn't grow up with cameras on me. It wasn't until my twenties that I became exposed to that level of scrutiny, and at that age, I wasn't mature enough to handle it. People commented on everything. They hated my clothes, thought I was stuck-up, questioned where my eyebrows were, and claimed my lips weren't real. Some even called me a con artist, a grifter, and a faker who only wanted fame and used my family's last name to get it. Commenters criticized my weight, speculated constantly about whether I was pregnant, and told me I wasn't a real mother because I had only one child. I've been told numerous times I wasn't a true Christian and have had every mistake I made pointed out. Fake accounts were made pretending to be me, and I had to go on the *Today* show to clear my name because some crazy woman made a claim that I was having an affair with an older man.[3]

I've had friends turn on me. People I thought I could trust sold lies about me to tabloids for a few extra bucks. After Dillon and I were married, we were followed by paparazzi to Mexico for our honeymoon. I've even been followed by paparazzi at my local grocery store. I've been put through the ringer. I can't imagine what it would be like to be insanely famous. *No thank you!*

Then someone on Reddit came up with a brutal nickname for me: "Famy" (famous + Amy). Although it's not the best nickname out there, I totally get how someone thought they were being clever to come up with it. But let me remind you of this: You have to realize how easily editing can distort reality. Producers had a significant role in shaping how I was portrayed. They were always telling me how to act and the kind of emotion they wanted to draw from certain scenes.

They wanted something funny and off-the-wall, so that's what I gave them. Producers and editors have a powerful ability to craft any type of narrative, and they can make anyone fit the story line. They can manipulate scenes, splice together conversations, and create the image they want. News flash: Reality TV isn't actually real. Episodes are carefully curated to maximize dramatic impact and viewer engagement, often at the expense of the individuals involved.

When I was constantly bombarded with negative judgments from strangers about myself, it was hard not to internalize some of that negativity or even lash out occasionally. Cyberbullying has been rough. It got to the point where my husband would first read the emails and delete the rude and hurtful ones. I've had enough name-calling in my life to last a lifetime, and the last thing I need is a bitter person hiding behind their computer screen, spreading malicious lies and false information and making fun of every move I make. It's bizarre to think that my life is under a magnifying glass for some strange, hateful person out there. The constant scrutiny and judgment can feel humiliating.

Over the years I've heard some truly ridiculous accusations, such as a rumor that I had my cousin James's love child. Um, *no*!

There's also some confusion around the name Duggar. The truth is, I was born a Duggar because my mom was single when she had me, so she gave me her last name. When I was nineteen, my parents got married, but I was a legal adult, so I kept the Duggar last name. When I got married, Duggar became my maiden name and I took Dillon's last name—King.

Another persistent rumor swirled around a stage name some record producers gave me when I was offered a contract at the age of twenty-two. "Amy Jordyn" was proposed to me by a country music label out of Nashville. It was confusing to fans because my aunt and uncle have a daughter named Jordyn, so there was online speculation about some connection between my cousin and the proposed stage name. Though I had no power over what fans believed, I knew that the story behind the recording contract was much deeper than just a name change.

It took time, but I no longer let those accusations, speculations, and lies bring me down. If you ask me, I'm in good company. Jesus was hated and misunderstood. Yet despite all the negativity he faced, he remained true to himself and his mission. I'm determined to do the same. I will continue to be myself and ignore all the hatred out there. I refuse to add to it; instead, I choose to rise above the negativity and focus on spreading positivity and kindness.

Don't let the opinions of strangers define your worth. Everyone has hidden insecurities. Instead, foster encouragement because a simple compliment can create ripples of positivity. Social media can be hurtful, but it can also connect us in wonderful ways. Let's use it to build one another up rather than tear one another down.

Despite the negativity, my character grew in popularity as the television show climbed the charts, and I began to receive offers for other shows like *Big Brother* and *Dancing with the Stars* (an automatic no, since dancing was forbidden!).

Producers used to ask me, "What kind of show do you want?" It was a complicated question. Did I really *want* my own show? I was already busy and trying to keep everyone happy.

"What else do you like to do?" was another tough question, one I answered with, "I love to sing." When the producers heard that, they started working on a television show about me pursuing a career as a recording artist in Nashville, singing with the biggest and brightest country music stars. I wasn't quite sure what to think. It would be nice to step into my own career after appearing for years on *19 Kids and Counting*, but I'd always dreamed of other things, like being a host of a show or just settling down as a wife and mother—my ultimate dream. How did country music artist fit?

Even though the Duggar show portrayed me as an adventurous girl always on the go, I've never been one to chase fame. In reality, I've always loved shopping at thrift stores or being at home—wearing no makeup, relaxing with my cat and an iced coffee while lounging on my sofa in sweatpants. Not exactly the high-octane life of a recording star on a tour bus somewhere on the highways of America.

My mom's dream had been to have a career in music. So the producers decided to film a special episode of *19 Kids and Counting* in which I traveled to Nashville to pursue my country music dream. I agreed, just to see what it would be like, and invited my mom and grandma to come with me. Once we were there, cameras followed me as I recorded several songs and worked with industry professionals. If everything worked out right, the producers told me I might have my own show, which would be a spin-off of *19 Kids and Counting*.

I can sing like a canary, but the producers wanted to make it look like I couldn't sing—like I was starting from scratch. When I did a beautiful take on a piece of music, they asked me to roll again and mess up the song so it would look like I was struggling. I sighed inwardly, disappointed at their portrayal of me: *Okay, it's clear that I'll be playing a role again. I thought this time would be different, that I'd portray myself the way I truly am. Seriously, why can't I be good at something on camera?*

But before I knew it, a top country music label showed strong interest in signing me to a deal, and I went with my producer to a high-rise building in downtown Nashville to meet with them. My mouth just about dropped open when I saw Dierks Bentley in the lobby.

"Hello, who are you?" he said, grabbing a cold beverage out of a refrigerator.

"Hi, Dierks. Nice to meet you. I'm Amy." What else was there to say?

After the crew filmed me singing for a group of executives for the episode, they left. I was invited to a special meeting, minus the cameras. My producer and I took an elevator ride to the twenty-seventh floor, where we walked into a large conference room full of people, every single one a male. There must have been twenty men in there with my male producer and me.

I immediately felt nervous. Where were the women? There didn't seem to be another female anywhere on the entire floor. The atmosphere in the room was charged, crackling with energy, and I grew more and more uncomfortable. I was just twenty-two years old, had never done anything like this before, and had no team of encouragers with me. My grandma and mom were waiting for me back at the hotel.

A huge stack of paper was set down in front of me—a recording contract. Everyone looked at me expectantly, but I knew I had better start reading so I understood what was being offered. First of all, they were offering me a lot of money. I wasn't an accountant, but the numbers seemed to add up to the potential for millions and millions of dollars. Wow, okay. I wasn't quite sure what to think about that.

But as I turned the pages and skimmed over the paragraphs, I was shocked at the amount of control I would be handing over to the record label. Just like all of us Duggars signed agreements to let our private lives be made public on television, including deeply personal moments in personal relationships, medical crises, or hospital treatments, signing this contract would mean yielding complete control of my life to a record company—where I could go, what I could do, what parties I'd be required to attend, whether I could talk about religion or who I voted for (that is, not at all), when or where I could get married, when or if I could have babies, where I'd be traveling and touring, "friends" I'd be required to spend time with, what I'd wear, the color of my hair, the perfect weight I had to aim for . . . I had to stop reading. It was clear I would be signing over virtually complete control of my personal life in return for a chance at a music career. The record company would tear me down, re-create me, sell my image and performance to the public, and require me to go along with all their decisions. In return for boatloads of money (supposedly), I would be owned.

A debate raged inside me. I already felt that so much was demanded of me, that my life wasn't really my own. But an opportunity like this was a dream, something so many people were chasing. And then there was the money! I wouldn't have to scrounge anymore to pay my bills and try to plan for the future. I'd have a fat bank account and my own career.

But out of nowhere came a quiet thought: *This sounds awful.* I hesitated, though. I felt the pressure of the men around me. I sensed they wanted control. I felt like a target, a piece of meat. I was outnumbered—no match for all the power in that room.

Then came an inner voice whispering, *Don't sign it.*

I put down the pen and looked up. And with a shaky voice I said, "I'm not going to sign it."

Someone in the room responded, "A million other girls would sign this in a heartbeat."

I took a quick breath, looked around at the disgruntled and frustrated faces, and made my decision. "Then choose them," I said. I stood up.

"Are you sure?" my producer asked with no small measure of intensity.

"I've never been more sure of anything in my life."

We were quickly ushered out of the room, into the elevator, and out of the building. My country music career was over before it ever really began, and "Amy Jordyn" was retired before she ever had a chance to shine. I was starting to see how money, power, and control had a dark side. Sure, my name would have been in the lights. I would have had fans, opened for huge stars, had money for a new wardrobe, plus a glam team, but at what cost? I would have been a shell of a person. A well-known Bible verse from Matthew's gospel danced through my head: "What good will it be for someone to gain the whole world, yet forfeit their soul?" (16:26).

SIXTEEN

Breaking Point

People have asked over the years, "Amy, were there any unmistakable signs that a colossal storm was brewing? Did you have any inkling of the magnitude of what was to come?"

I did, but only after I discovered some unexpected computer files.

My dad decided to buy an old computer from Josh, who always had the newest tech. One day I was searching around trying to get familiar with the new computer when I saw under the menu button a tab labeled "Josh's Files." I clicked on it out of curiosity. What I saw completely horrified me—thousands of pornographic photos and videos of both women and men.

As fast as I could, I grabbed Scotch tape and several sheets of black construction paper to put over the screen. I then moved all the files to the trash folder. I didn't want to permanently delete them, because this was proof that what I saw was real. I was used to people doubting me, and this was hard evidence no one could deny.

I was disgusted by what I saw, but in a way, I also felt a strange sense of relief knowing that Josh wasn't a robot. You must realize I never once witnessed him, even remotely, being defiant or disobedient toward his parents. Yet porn and masturbation were in direct conflict with the beliefs of his family and certainly IBLP.

During the filming of *19 Kids and Counting*, Josh came across as a natural-born leader who radiated kindness. In all aspects, he appeared to epitomize the ideal first son. Obviously, I was beyond shocked that Mr. Perfect harbored a dark secret like this. I always assumed there might be more to him than met the eye. After seeing the quantity of videos I discovered, I had to believe he had an addiction and, due to the nature of the videos, serious mental problems as well. I went back and forth on what I should do. There in the trash folder was the evidence I needed for my uncle to believe me—maybe for the first time in his life. I knew I wouldn't be taken seriously if I had no proof.

I showed my mom the trash folder on my dad's computer before I permanently deleted the files. She called Jim Bob immediately, and we told him what we saw, describing the images in detail—including orgy videos and rough abusive scenes where women were being beaten and peed on. Glancing at the videos as I deleted them, it was clear that some had been downloaded and that Josh had deliberately saved clips of his favorite scenes, carefully edited to his liking. Just thinking about what I saw still makes me want to throw up.

Jim Bob immediately wanted to talk to me, but I put the call on the speaker so my mom could hear. He said in a calm and casual voice, "Amy, you must have been mistaken. My son does not have a problem with pornography. Josh would shield his eyes from such sinful images." Completely in denial, he continued, "He bought that computer from a guy at a pawnshop, so there's no telling what you'll find there."

I responded with one question: "Uncle Jim Bob, if what you are telling me is correct, then why did I find all of this pornography under the folder name Josh's Files?"

My uncle went silent. A few seconds later, stumbling through his words, he told me I was simply wrong and hung up the phone.

Unfortunately, I wasn't surprised by my uncle's reaction. During family gatherings, I've always been the one shrugged off as though my thoughts didn't matter. It wasn't just about whether I was right or wrong; it seemed like my family had a collective agreement to not take me seriously—no matter how hard I tried to explain myself. This wasn't something that happened a handful of times; it happened over and over again, which made me feel completely dismissed, as though I was present but unseen, as though my voice was just background noise—heard but never truly acknowledged. The more I experienced this, the more I started to believe that maybe I really *was* the problem, that no matter what I said or did, I would never be enough in their eyes.

As the years passed, it became the norm to feel like I was on the outside looking in. While everyone else seemed to fit in perfectly, there I was, standing on the other side of the fence. As happened with most things in my family, this pivotal issue with Josh was swept under the rug, buried beneath layers of silence and denial. It was painfully clear to both my mom and me that my uncle was attempting to lock up the secret as tightly as he could.

In a moment of clarity, I saw through the shiny happy facade and suddenly knew that my cousin's holier-than-thou persona was nothing more than an act. Josh, the one who was always the first to stand in front of a crowd and loudly sing hymns, the one to have every single piece of hair in place and show off the brightest smile, clearly had a real problem. But my hands were tied. Nobody would listen to Crazy Cousin Amy. And the truth remained locked away.

Then a year later, something happened that rocked me.

Uncle Jim Bob's big house was buzzing with the kind of joy that fills the air during a big celebration. Kids were everywhere, laughter ringing, as another family member was about to be born. Amid the celebration, I went into the huge pantry to grab some more napkins. When I opened the door, a faint cry caught my ear. As the merriment continued in the living room, there behind one of the deep freezers was one of my teen cousins. She was curled up in a fetal position, rocking back and forth, desperately trying to stifle her sobs. One hand over her mouth and the other clenching her long denim skirt, her face stained with makeup, clearly suffering, she was trying to be as silent as she could.

This was the same kind of silent suffering I was all too familiar with, and I immediately responded with empathy. Without a second thought, I got down on my knees, whispered her name, and held her as tightly as I could. I thought that maybe if I said her name, I might be able to gently remind her of who she was and that I saw her.

Tears streaming down her face, she trembled in my arms and proceeded to completely fall apart. I wrapped my arms around her and just held her. For a moment time stood still. As the napkins lay forgotten on the floor, my thoughts raced. This was my cousin, someone I thought I knew; yet as I embraced her, I didn't even recognize this person.

In the aftermath of that pantry encounter, questions swirled in my mind. Why was my cousin in the throes of a panic attack and hiding in the pantry? What shadows lurked behind those terrified eyes? What caused this dreadful pain?

A few days later, I approached her to ask if we could chat privately. She seemed a bit puzzled by the request, her radiant smile and bright eyes giving no clues about what I was about to hear. With genuine concern, I assured her of my support, offering to be a safe space and a lifeline if she needed it.

Her response, almost robotic, came as a surprise. "I appreciate your kind words, Amy, but I don't know what you're talking about."

My heart immediately sank. My eyes began to tear up as I whispered, "You don't remember when I held you on the pantry floor? You seemed to be right in the middle of an intense panic attack, like something awful had happened."

She looked at me, smiling so sweetly, and said, "Nothing comes to mind. I think I'm needed in the kitchen. I better go. Love you, Ames."

I stood there in shock. I've always been aware that IBLP teaches that having any emotions other than happiness and a quiet spirit is considered sinful, but this level of denial was something new. *If she's had one breakdown, curled up in the corner of a pantry, how many more has she had?* I wondered. My heart ached for her. I made it my mission to try to figure out what was going on and get her some help. However, I knew that professional help wasn't allowed in my family. My best option was to tell her parents that I thought she was going through something difficult.

After my cousin and I had talked, I walked back to the big living room where the other kids were. I looked around with new eyes at the kids playing, some singing by the piano, others chasing one another outside, some of the girls making homemade bread, and some of the boys playing chess. As I watched, I wondered, *Who else is silently hurting?*

A few days later, I told my aunt Michelle about what I had witnessed in the pantry—such deep pain and hurt in my cousin, who was unable to articulate why she was upset. Aunt Michelle was sweet as pie but completely dismissive. I might as well have been talking to a brick wall.

After that failed attempt, I tried talking to Uncle Jim Bob about it, but his phone must have been more interesting than our conversation. It felt like I was shouting into the void, my words and concerns bouncing off, unheard and unacknowledged. The more I tried, the more I hit a dead end. My frustration grew, and I began to wonder why my attempt to share my account of what I had witnessed in the pantry wasn't a priority to anyone.

Do they know something I don't?

Eventually I stopped trying to find answers, not because I didn't care—I cared so deeply—but because I felt helpless. That decision to let it go still causes me to choke up to this day.

Over time, I found myself confused, even a bit embarrassed for even entertaining the notion that something could be off. After all, this was America's favorite family—so loving, godly, and inspirational in their dedication to maintaining a healthy family structure. Who was I to call that into question? I would be lying if I said I didn't struggle with the thoughts that kept creeping into my head. I wondered if I was delusional, and if so, what was wrong with me. Why would my mind jump to such dramatic conclusions so readily?

I questioned myself repeatedly, so much so that I began to think I was inherently flawed and dreadfully separated from God. What was it about me that made me the perpetual outsider in my own family? They all seemed perfectly happy, so why did I have this uneasiness deep inside me? Why did my mind spiral into such darkness? The thoughts kept me up at night, making me doubt my own intuition. I began to wonder if the problem wasn't the world around me, but me.

As much as those dreadful doubts gnawed at me, I couldn't shake the nagging feeling that there had to be more to it. There had to be something deeper at play, some underlying dynamic in the family that I couldn't quite grasp. Only later would I find out that, yes, something troubling was definitely going on.

SEVENTEEN

Righteous Rage

For a while I silenced my inner doubts, convincing myself that I was overthinking things and had nothing to be concerned about. It may seem absurd now, but at the time, I had grown to respect and admire my family and couldn't bear the thought of being the one who might tarnish their pristine image. I loved them and looked up to them; after all, we were family, and family sticks together, no matter what. I held on to an idealized vision of what a perfect family looked like, and in my mind, that family was mine. Other than the moment in the pantry with my cousin and finding porn on Josh's computer, my cousins seemed flawless in every way. They excelled in every pursuit they embarked on. They were morally upright and pure. Money flowed abundantly. There were no issues to contend with, seemingly no skeletons lurking in the family closet. They walked the walk of an ideal family.

The Duggar name was special, squeaky-clean, and to fit in, I intended to do my part to keep it that way. My contractual duty to keep filming with the family helped motivate me to maintain a great relationship with them. I had already caused ripples by probing and asking questions, and the last thing I wanted was to create more waves. I buried my suspicions, hoping they'd fade into the background, attempted to stay in my family's good graces, and tried to navigate the delicate balance between loyalty and truth in a way that would allow me to sleep at night.

One day, however, an ordinary trip to Walmart turned into a nightmare, a defining moment that will live in my memory forever. As I approached the checkout counter, my eyes absentmindedly scanned the magazine rack. Magazines, usually just a blur of glossy covers and sensational headlines, didn't typically capture my attention. But this day was different. There, amid the rack of publications, a single headline leapt out at me. In bold white letters it read, "HOUSE OF HORRORS."

I thought my heart was going to come right out of my chest. Time slowed to a crawl. As I stood by that counter, frozen in place, my eyes fixed on those ominous words as a chill ran down my spine. Tears gathered in my eyes until all I saw was a misty blur. I didn't know it then, but that headline marked the beginning of a journey into madness, unraveling secrets and truths that would forever alter the course of my life. But in that split second, all I could do was stand there and grapple with the weight of those three simple words—*House of Horrors*. The house they were talking about belonged to my family. The horrors concealed inside that home were scarier than I could have ever imagined, and the focus was on serious sexual abuse allegations against my beloved cousin Josh.

For at least fifteen minutes I stood there in disbelief as I read the article. This couldn't be my family, the people I knew and loved and whose house I had been in countless times in my life.

I had so many thoughts swirling in my mind:

Can this information be true?
What's going to happen next?
Could I have done more?

As soon as I got home, I called my mom, crying, mad, and sad, desperate for answers. I begged her to tell me if she had known about these accusations. Just as completely in the dark and confused as I was, she began to cry. We hoped and prayed that if something so horrifying was going on, her brother would choose to be honest.

Immediately, we called Uncle Jim Bob. He told us, "You know how those tabloids are. They're always making mountains out of molehills. Everything will get straightened out. Just don't talk to anyone; let it blow over." It felt like he was giving an interview instead of talking to family members. His response felt rehearsed, which worried us even more. It was like he had practiced for the moment when these awful truths would come to light.

Completely dumbfounded by his response, we knew he was headed for a gaping wound. His little Band-Aid was not going to be able to stop what was coming.

The next day was my wedding dress fitting, and my mom and grandma were there with me. I asked Grandma point-blank if she knew anything about Josh's scandal. She told us the girls were sleeping outside in a tent and Josh went into the tent to scare them. Then while they were sleeping, he accidentally touched them inappropriately. "It's no big deal, Amy."

I was shocked. Surely an innocent scare during a camping night wouldn't be headline news. I was more confused than ever. Things didn't add up; what I was being told wasn't believable. I had never felt more frustrated in my entire life. I asked myself, *What is the truth, and why is it always so hard to find?* As I stood in the store in my wedding dress, I cried—not because I was filled with happiness and looking forward to my big day, but because I was desperate for answers that no one seemed to want to provide.

From a young age, my uncle drilled into us the importance of truth. He would repeatedly tell his children and me that lying never works out for the best. "God can't stand a lying tongue," he'd say. He compared the act of lying to the effect of a snowball rolling down a hill: It starts out small, but as more snow (more lies) is added to cover the initial ball (lie), the snowball grows uncontrollably as it rolls down the hill, gathering size and momentum until it's impossible to stop the gigantic mess that has been created.

The irony of his metaphor was something I would come to understand much later. Uncle Jim Bob taught us to fear lies, yet I couldn't help but think that he built his whole world on deception.

As the scandal unfolded, the shock was overwhelming. It hit like a wave we never saw coming. In the midst of my wedding preparations in early spring 2015, life turned upside down. As I was getting fitted for my wedding dress, excited for the future, a text came through to my mom from one of her friends: **Turn on the TV**. The moment we did, our hearts sank. The screen was filled with headlines about Josh's misconduct toward his sisters. I was in shock. I couldn't comprehend what I was seeing. My cousin, someone I had once looked up to, had lived a lie right in front of us.

What made it all the more painful, beyond the horrific nature of what had happened, was that we were finding out the truth along with the rest of the world. This was supposed to be my time of joy, and instead I was watching everything unravel. Every channel replayed the story on loop. I remember looking at my mom, who was utterly heartbroken, tears streaming down her face as I held her close. It felt like the floor had dropped out from beneath us.

May 2015: *In Touch Weekly* published police reports from 2006 revealing that Josh Duggar had molested five underage girls between 2002 and 2003, when he was fourteen to fifteen years old.[4] Four of the victims were his younger sisters, and one was a family babysitter.

According to the reports, Josh inappropriately touched the girls, sometimes while they slept, targeting their breasts and genital areas over and under their clothing.

The incidents came to light in 2003 when Jim Bob Duggar, Josh's father, learned about the behavior. Rather than immediately contacting authorities, the family handled the situation internally. Jim Bob reportedly consulted with church elders and eventually arranged for Josh to receive counseling at a Christian program in Little Rock, Arkansas. This "counseling" primarily consisted of physical labor and mentoring from a family friend, who was a home remodeler, not a counselor.

Josh was never formally charged or prosecuted for these acts. By the time police officially investigated in 2006 (prompted by a tip to a hotline), the statute of limitations had expired. The investigation was triggered when Oprah Winfrey's production team received an anonymous email about the allegations before a scheduled appearance by the family, and they forwarded this information to authorities.

The police report was ultimately ordered sealed to protect the identities of the minors involved. However, when *In Touch* obtained it through a Freedom of Information Act request in 2015, they published a redacted version.

In the aftermath of these revelations, Josh resigned from his position at the Family Research Council, and TLC suspended and later canceled *19 Kids and Counting*, the reality show featuring the Duggar family.[5]

How could this have happened? How could someone who was supposed to be a role model, a person of integrity, choose deceit over honesty? The fact that my uncle had looked us all in the eyes and denied any wrongdoing—how do we recover from that? The pain wasn't just in the truth coming to light; it was in the years of lies we had unknowingly lived. Every time we visited their house, every shared meal, every casual conversation in which my uncle pretended to be the good, righteous man we all believed he was, helped nurture and grow this huge lie we participated in without even realizing it. It was one thing for the world to be shocked, but for us to discover such a profound betrayal in real time felt like a wound that cut unimaginably deeper. I couldn't believe that this man we trusted, who stood for faith and family, had lied to our faces.

I felt sick thinking about every birthday we celebrated, every baby we welcomed into the world, every moment that was supposed to be pure, filled with family and faith. Every time my mom and her brother shared lunch, every time a camera pointed in our direction for the world to see our "perfect" family, it was nothing but a mask, a lie that concealed the real truth of the disgusting betrayal that had been festering beneath the surface. How could Uncle Jim Bob do that to us? How could he preach about faith, about morality, when he had been living a lie the entire time?

Fed up with being kept in the dark, a couple of weeks later, I made a bold decision: If no one was going to tell me what the heck was happening, I was going to uncover the truth myself. With a fire burning in my stomach, I set off, determined to get to the bottom of things.

As I drove to my uncle's house, a new question popped up in my head with every mile. The rage went a little deeper, and my heart broke a little more. This time, there was no turning back. As I stepped inside the home, a heavy atmosphere greeted me that felt like a suffocating blanket. The older girls were all gathered in a circle, somber, shoulders hunched and downcast eyes speaking volumes.

Without a word, I approached the group and gently tapped one of them on the shoulder, requesting permission to join their huddle. I hugged them all tightly, and tears flowed furiously and freely at the weight of the situation and the uncertainty of the future. In a strange way, I felt a sense of gratitude. At that moment, they were letting me in, allowing me to be with them, and letting me share in their pain. For the first time in my life, I was allowed to be in their inner circle in a way I had never been before.

I hadn't headed to my cousins' house merely to offer comfort though. I was there on a mission to confront Josh. When I found him, he was holed up in an RV about forty feet from the side door of the big house. After storming through the yard and opening the door without even knocking, I came face-to-face with him. He was sitting on the couch with Anna by his side, and they were lovingly holding hands. I get the idea of a spouse standing by their partner through thick and thin, but if Josh had truly done what he was accused of doing, how could anyone excuse his behavior, even his wife?

I felt a surge of righteous anger coursing through my veins. I looked directly into his eyes, my gaze burning with intensity, and demanded to know how long his abusive behavior had been going on. He gave no response, simply keeping his eyes glued to the floor, avoiding my piercing stare.

Then I screamed, "When did this start?"

Josh again stayed silent.

Now, at the top of my lungs, I shouted, "Josh, how come you never did anything to me?"

His refusal to speak only fueled the frustration.

At this point I was seeing red.

"Why didn't you touch *me*? I *wish* you would have tried to put your moves on me. I wish you would *have tried*. I would have kicked your ass! I would have called the police. I would have made it where you couldn't have children. I would have *stopped* you. You are nothing but a *monster!*"

I knew that if Josh tried something with me, I was strong enough to defend myself against him. I would have been able to fight back, expose him, and make sure he was unable to do something like this to anyone else. I could've protected my sweet girl cousins.

Finally, after what seemed like an eternity of silence, he looked up and said, "I knew better."

As I continued to stare directly into his eyes, slowly a smile spread across his face. It was the kind of smile that sent shivers down my spine, a twisted grin that was unlocking a world of chaos, suffering, and pain that was yet to come for my family. It was the creepiest smile I had ever seen.

Just as the tension reached its peak, Uncle Jim Bob barged in with his usual attempts to defuse a situation. He was entirely too calm, and in a condescending tone he said, "Now, Amy, let's not stir up contempt."

Still furious and with my pulse racing, I couldn't help but roll my eyes at his ridiculous attempt to brush aside the gravity of the moment. His son was a predator, and yet he was more worried about my language and tone of voice. I was outraged! I slammed the door behind me as I stormed out, yelling as loudly as I could in the once-peaceful front yard of the Duggar family compound, "This is bull****!"

I drove off, leaving behind the sickening atmosphere that once commanded my respect. I needed to process. I needed room to breathe and organize my mind, which was racing in countless directions. I knew I needed to find a peaceful place to unwind. Leaving wasn't just a choice; it was a necessity for my own mental health. This was one of the first times in my life that I decided to put myself first.

As I drove down the road, I began to feel more like a superhero than the crazy, irrational, wild girl that my family had convinced me I was. It was as if I had a cape billowing behind me as I soared to new heights of self-assurance. For the first time, my voice rang out loud and clear! They may not have liked it, but they sure heard me.

It was a transformative experience, a pivotal moment in which I embraced the power that God gave me to stand up for what was right. I felt a surge of confidence growing inside me. This new version of Amy was unapologetically bold and fearless, and I knew there was no going back. With each passing mile, I grew more determined in my commitment to become the best version of myself, untethered by the constraints of fear and control. I was becoming a truth teller. I was taking my first steps toward becoming a holy disruptor.

CHAPTER
EIGHTEEN

The Price of Control

This is the part of my story where pride comes before a fall (Proverbs 16:18).

While my mother was shattered by the news, my grandmother, surprisingly, seemed unmoved. She calmly insisted this whole thing was a misunderstanding, that Jim Bob had assured her it was just a scare. She believed that the story had been exaggerated, claiming Josh had simply gotten too close to the girls during a backyard campout. But even as she spoke, I knew in my heart it wasn't the whole truth. I couldn't fathom how a minor incident could make national headlines. But my grandmother, ever loyal to the family narrative and quick to sweep horrible things under the rug, stood firm. She insisted it was nothing more than an innocent mistake. I wanted to believe her, but the gnawing feeling in my gut told me there was more to the story that was covered up in the name of saving face.

My uncle's struggle with trust and telling the truth became painfully obvious. It was like he had built a wall around himself, and no one could penetrate it. The guy who used to be so approachable now felt miles away, even when he was right in front of you.

It's sad to see someone you love lose the best parts of themselves to something as empty as money, status, and power. It's a real-life lesson on the Bible's teaching that "the love of money is a root of all kinds of evil" (1 Timothy 6:10). The way I see it, money didn't just change Uncle Jim Bob's behavior; it changed his identity. The trust, the warmth, the genuine connection he used to offer—all of that got lost somewhere along the way. Watching this transformation play out, especially when I remember who this man used to be, makes me realize that money can take a good person and twist them into something unrecognizable.

The worst part for me was realizing how skillfully he had played us all. In my opinion, he had fooled everyone—family members, viewers, even the network and film crew—with his mask of family loyalty and Christian values. But I believe that beneath that polished surface lay a man who would do anything to protect his reputation, even if it meant fundamentally ignoring Josh's crimes. When Josh's behavior spiraled out of control, instead of getting him the help I was told he had been begging for from church elders and other IBLP members, my uncle did virtually nothing. Josh's obsession festered in secrecy, feeding on the darkness, because it was easier to keep those secrets than it was to face the truth. And all the while, I believed that my uncle covered it up, creating the illusion of a perfect family life around him, fooling everyone into thinking he was the epitome of family values.

It dawned on me that I had been kept out of the inner circle on purpose. My uncle knew I was perceptive and that I could sense something was wrong. Keeping me at arm's length was his way of preventing the truth from getting out. If I had been allowed to stay overnight, maybe I would have caught Josh sneaking into the girls' bedrooms sooner and could have intervened. Meanwhile, the truly crazy one—the one quoting Scripture, smiling for the cameras, helping the elderly, and portraying himself as the ideal family man—was hiding in plain sight. He let Josh's sickness fester, turning a blind eye while the abuse and secrecy carried on—all to protect his own selfish interests. That's what I believe in my heart. It's my opinion, and I've learned that it's okay to say it out loud. We're all entitled to our own beliefs, and they *do* matter.

My grandma later told me that Josh had begged for help, again and again, confessing to a problem I was told didn't exist. He finally admitted to a struggle with porn. Young, desperate, and lost, he didn't know how to cope or change his behavior. So the addiction took root, growing and festering inside him until it completely consumed him. Now, looking at his mug shot, I barely recognize him. He looks so different from the cousin, the Joshy, I grew up with. Who is that man smiling back? That's what any addiction does—it escalates, deepens, and ultimately destroys everything in its path. But my uncle is also to blame. He allowed Josh's sickness to grow unchecked, letting the cycle of abuse and secrecy continue because of his own selfish interests.

I firmly believe that my aunt and uncle failed Josh. Their approach to parenting wasn't really parenting at all. It's perfectly okay to have rules and guidelines for your children, but when your child comes to you and tells you he's having a problem, you listen. You act swiftly and decisively to do what's best for *your children*, not what's best for your image. Instead, they allowed Josh to remain in the house in full awareness of what he was capable of, while the girls were forced to smile, forgive quickly, and bury their trauma. My cousins weren't allowed to receive professional counseling, which could have made a world of difference in their healing. Instead, the girls spoke with their mom—my aunt Michelle. She probably tried her best to help them work through the trauma, but they needed much more than that.

I did speak to the fifth victim, who is not related to the Duggar family. I talked to her for a good hour and told her how sorry I was about what had happened to her. She told me she is moving on and ready for a quieter life, and that she's in a much better place now. I have mad respect for a woman like that.

Josh, on the other hand, was barely held accountable for his actions, which is exactly why he was later caught in yet another heartbreaking scandal. The shock hit us all hard.

August 2015: Josh Duggar became entangled in the Ashley Madison scandal when hackers released user data from the website, which marketed itself as a service for people seeking extramarital affairs. Josh was identified among the site's users when his personal information, including credit card details and two paid accounts, was exposed in the data breach.

The revelation came just three months after TLC had suspended *19 Kids and Counting* following reports that Josh had molested five girls as a teen. According to the leaked data, Josh had paid nearly $1,000 for two Ashley Madison subscriptions between February 2013 and May 2015, a period during which he was married, had children, and was working as the executive director of the Family Research Council's political action committee, a conservative lobbying group that advocated for traditional family values.

Josh publicly confessed to infidelity on August 20, 2015, admitting in a statement, "I have been the biggest hypocrite ever. While espousing faith and family values, I have been unfaithful to my wife. . . . I have secretly over the last several years been viewing pornography on the internet and this became a secret addiction."[6]

The consequences were swift but largely personal rather than legal, as adultery itself is not typically criminally prosecuted. Josh resigned from his position at the Family Research Council, and TLC permanently canceled *19 Kids and Counting*. He subsequently entered a faith-based rehabilitation facility called Reformers Unanimous in Rockford, Illinois, where he reportedly spent six months.[7]

The scandal severely damaged Josh's public reputation and caused significant distress to his family, particularly his wife, Anna, who nonetheless remained married to him despite the public humiliation. And the victims—my cousins and a person who visited my cousins' house frequently—are rarely mentioned.

We had already weathered one storm, believing that the worst was finally behind us, only to find out Josh had been living a double life. None of us saw it coming. We thought he was working to change, to rebuild trust. He had even written letters to several people in the family asking for prayer and forgiveness. But then came the Ashley Madison scandal—his name exposed among thousands from a hacked site designed to help married people find affairs.

It was a devastating blow. He had cheated on his wife, Anna, who was pregnant with their fourth child. How low could one possibly go? I looked at his name on that list, and I couldn't reconcile it with the cousin I thought I knew. We were left with so many questions, and the whole thing felt disturbing. Josh had always seemed so smart, yet he had made reckless choices. He used a famous deejay's photo as his profile picture and used my grandma's address to create the account. How careless and disrespectful could he be?

In the end, we couldn't help but question everything. How much more was hidden beneath the surface? It was a painful realization that Josh's problems ran deeper than we could see or understand. And seeing his face in the headlines again, knowing how much pain this would bring to everyone who loved him, was heartbreaking. In my opinion, Josh wasn't sorry for what he had done; he was sorry he got caught. That's what made it all the more difficult to watch. How can someone express remorse when they've never really been forced to face the consequences of their actions? There was no real accountability. His parents covered for him, which is why he never changed. That's a reality I simply cannot support.

I know there isn't a perfect parent guideline, but here's what I would have done: I would have removed Josh from the home immediately, making sure he wouldn't be able to hurt or be tempted to hurt anyone else. I would have let the authorities handle the situation, even if it meant taking him to juvenile jail. It wouldn't have been easy, but I would have done it because it's what's right. When he got out, I would have made sure he received intensive therapy to address the root causes of his issues, not just a slap on the wrist and a half-hearted attempt at rehabilitation.

My uncle did send Josh away multiple times to an IBLP correction program, where he was surrounded by troubled guys like himself. I'm not sure why IBLP produced so many young men who needed serious help, but I have my thoughts. Of course a teenage boy is going to be curious—it's human nature. That's why sex education is essential. If we don't teach them, they'll act on that curiosity without understanding or guidance. We can't expect a young person to figure everything out on the way to the honeymoon suite, merely by watching a DVD about the birds and the bees. Their education must be not just about sex itself but also about self-control, respect, and how to handle their desires in a healthy and godly way. Otherwise, they are only being set up for failure.

IBLP seems to be a breeding ground for lust, confusion, and shame. In my opinion, they do nothing to help teen boys and young men walk in wisdom. Josh's involvement in the program came during the period of time when he seemed to disappear often, and we were told his "big heart" had led him to go on a mission trip or help people recover from a destructive hurricane. Many times, I questioned where Josh was. No one seemed to be bothered that he wasn't around for many of the family gatherings and trips.

As a young teen, he asked for help, but I believe it never really came, at least not in the way he truly needed it. You don't become a deceitful or deeply disturbed person overnight. So I've always wondered, *What really happened to Josh?* That question haunts me to this day. I believe there's so much more to the story, layers we may never uncover. And honestly, I'm not sure we'll ever get the full truth.

In a way, I have some compassion for Josh—a *very* small amount. As a teen, he confessed to his dad and the church elders that something was seriously wrong. It was a moment of honesty when he asked for help. But he never truly received it. It wasn't just Uncle Jim Bob who overlooked such trauma; it was also his friends. Jim Bob's mentor and lifelong friend was accused by his daughter, after his death, of having abused her. Uncle Jim Bob's longtime best friend lost custody of his minor children and was accused of a pattern of abuse of the children.[8] A trustworthy source close to IBLP has shared stories about fathers in that organization who are sick and perverted. So if Josh went to elders of the church who may have been committing crimes in their own families, what type of advice would they have given Josh? Would they have helped cover up his sin, like they helped cover up each other's?

It makes me sick to think about what has happened to Josh and how far he has fallen. But here's the thing: While I can understand how he got to where he is, the damage he caused by the choices he made can't be erased. He is still responsible for his actions. I don't condone the disgusting things he looked at or his betrayal of his wife. But when you look at how his parents handled—or rather, ignored—the problem, it's not hard to see why things spiraled out of control. They had a chance to intervene, to help him, to stop the darkness from growing, but instead, they let it worsen over time. They let it go unchecked. Now everyone is paying the price, especially the victims—my sweet, innocent cousins, along with another teen female and Josh's wife and kids, as well as, according to Phil McGraw (Dr. Phil), quite likely many more.[9]

CHAPTER
NINETEEN

A Greedy Heart

June 9, 2019, is etched into my memory forever as the worst day of my life (and that's saying a lot). It was a Sunday like any other. My mom had invited me over to swim and have a cookout, but I was exhausted from the weekend. I decided to relax on the couch instead and told her I'd take a rain check on the invite. She said she'd call me back later, but the call never came. Instead, late in the afternoon, my phone rang. I assumed it was my grandma, as usual, but to my surprise, it was my uncle Jim Bob. He never called just to chat, so I knew something was off.

With an unsettling calmness in his voice, he said, "It's a nice day, isn't it?"

"Yeah," I replied, anxiety already creeping into my chest.

Then came the words that would change everything. "I don't like telling you this over the phone, but Grandma passed away today." His delivery was cold, robotic, devoid of any emotion.

I screamed out in disbelief, "WHAT! NO, NO, NO, NO!"

But his response was the same—detached and matter-of-fact. "I'm sorry. It's true."

The phone slipped from my hands as I collapsed onto the floor, shaking uncontrollably. I lay there for hours, unable to comprehend what had just happened. The woman I spoke to multiple times a day, my confidante, my best friend, was gone. Just like that, without any warning, without a chance to say goodbye. I learned later that my mom was the one who found her in the pool. My heart ached for my dear mom.

In the days that followed, I dreaded her upcoming funeral. I didn't want to attend. It wasn't just the overwhelming grief that made me want to keep me away; it was the spectacle I knew it would become. My grandma had always been humble, preferring simplicity over extravagance, and I knew she would have wanted a quiet, private service.

But as expected, my uncle turned it into a grand production. The funeral was televised. It became another performance, another opportunity for the family to uphold their public image rather than honor her in a way that truly reflected her life. Standing there, surrounded by people who had no idea of the raw turmoil behind the scenes, I felt angry. My grandma deserved more than this. She deserved peace, something none of us seemed capable of finding in this family of secrets.

It reminded me of the episode that featured my grandpa's birthday. He was critically ill because of a brain tumor and had lost a ton of weight. Uncle Jim Bob wheeled him out to where the family had gathered to wish him a happy birthday. As he slumped over in his chair, practically nonresponsive, my cousins were forced to celebrate. You could see the extreme confusion and uncomfortableness in their eyes on this anything but festive occasion. Grandpa looked like he was on his deathbed.

Reflecting on these events, it's clear that the very principles we were taught were violated by those who preached them. From my perspective, my uncle built his life on lies, and the consequences of those deceptions reverberated through the entire family. My mom and Jim Bob were supposed to do all the funeral arrangements together. The will was already locked down. But my mom discovered my uncle had set up other meetings and discussed other arrangements without inviting her.

I was invited to sit in the front row at the funeral with my aunt and uncle, clearly because of my deep connection to my grandmother. When one of the girls gave a eulogy, I wanted to laugh at the irony. Her speech was full of praise for my grandma, but it felt hollow coming from someone who had spent such little quality time with her.

Since I was not a regular cast member of the new spin-off Duggar reality show *Counting On*, which began airing in December 2015, it was as though my presence at the funeral had been erased. Apparently, my grief and my special connection to my grandma were no longer valuable. So even though I was present, I was edited out of the funeral special, as was my mom and Dillon. I told my mom, "Well, now that Grandma isn't here to stand up for us, I guess we'll see how things shake out in the family." It was clear that the family dynamics would shift, and not for the better. We were left to navigate a world in which appearances took precedence over genuine care and respect.

A few days after the funeral, my mom and Jim Bob finally received the details of the trust. Jim Bob, who was the executor, had promised my grandma that he would always look after his sister. But oh, how brotherly love truly revealed itself. My uncle had the audacity to tell my mom, "Deanna, you can have whatever you want from Mom's house, but I need you to move out in four days." Four days to pack up a life, before the dust had a chance to settle, just moments after her immeasurably great loss! What kind of man does that?

My mom called me sobbing. She was crying so hard I could barely understand her. She was beyond overwhelmed. We scrambled to pack up as much as we could, hoping and praying that by some miracle we would be able to get everything done. Thankfully, my uncle agreed to extend the deadline by a few days, but the damage had already been done.

My mom walked around in a daze, utterly heartbroken. She had been Grandma's primary caregiver, spending every moment with her for more than three years. The day she discovered her mother's lifeless body in the pool was unfathomably difficult. The media called it an accidental drowning, but my mom knew the truth. Grandma had a stroke. It was something Jim Bob conveniently chose to ignore, avoiding an autopsy, even though he knew about my grandma's health issues.

After the trauma my mom endured, she was in no condition to deal with any of the complicated matters that followed. Feeling as though she were immersed in fog, she was barely holding it together, her mind stuck in that horrifying moment when she found her mother. The last thing she needed was more stress. In my mom's fragile state, Jim Bob demanded an extra $20,000 before transferring the deed to Grandma's investment properties—Mom's rightful inheritance. It was a blow my mom didn't see coming, and honestly, she didn't need to give him a dime. The demands for more money weren't even in the will. But with her mind elsewhere, she wasn't thinking clearly, and in my opinion, my uncle took full advantage of that.

Here's the thing: Her brother has more than enough money. So why ask for more? It felt like an unnecessary power play, a way for him to make things harder for my mom at a time when she was broken and numb. To my way of thinking, the fact that he chose that moment to twist the knife really showed his true colors. My mom handed over the keys to her home with hardly any money left in her bank account and no place to go. My uncle's actions added insult to injury and spoke volumes about how little he truly cared about her well-being.

In the midst of this turmoil, Jim Bob offered my mom a place to stay with him and his family, but on the condition that she would handle all the laundry for their household. I hated to see my mom going through this alone. I knew she needed support, and I missed her deeply. So I did what I thought a daughter should do and invited her to move in permanently with us. It wasn't just a way to help her; it was a balm for my soul. We did set one condition. If she wanted to live with us, she had to acknowledge and understand that this was a place of healing and rebuilding, not just a temporary refuge, and she needed to commit to this new journey without my dad, who couldn't seem to let her go. His abusive behavior toward her had continued to escalate, and I feared for her life if she were to continue to have contact with him.

So if Mom agreed to end the long and tortured relationship with my father, Dillon and I would provide a safe place for her to live and to heal, a place where she could rest and put the pieces back together. She accepted and quickly moved in.

TWENTY

Circle of Trust

Once the secrets behind the scandals had begun to unravel, I decided to stop going to the big house. Long before that, I had already chosen to step away from filming altogether. I was tired of being villainized, not being compensated for my time and talents, and being judged. It all became too much. Each season followed the same predictable story line—babies, weddings, and the antics of the "crazy cousin," who inevitably tried and failed.

As I reflect on my time with the show, one particular episode leaps out at me. It revolved around my birthday. Birthdays in the Duggar family were always a grand affair, with the house adorned with festive banners, laughter filling every corner, and the always massive cake waiting for us to enjoy. The local bakery must have loved us, because there always seemed to be a celebration, and along with it plenty of cake! It reminded me of my childhood birthday parties—large, lively, and filled with fun.

I had celebrated countless birthdays with my cousins, but this particular birthday was different. It's not easy to surprise me, but boy, was I ever taken aback. I remember driving to my cousins' house, anticipating another wonderful celebration. But as I opened the door, my heart nearly stopped when I was greeted by a clown on stilts. Everyone was laughing. Now, anyone who knows me well is aware that one of my biggest fears is clowns. My cousins, with their twisted sense of humor, had decided to exploit this fear to the fullest. They had scoured the internet to find the scariest clown images imaginable, printed them out, and glued them to paper plates to make masks. Everywhere I looked, grotesque clown faces popped out and scared me.

The cameras were rolling, capturing every moment of my horror. My heart was pounding so hard I thought it might burst. In an attempt to maintain some composure, I took many, many bathroom breaks. Behind the closed door, I had small panic attacks, hyperventilating and trying to calm my nerves. Each time I stepped back into the party, the fear would hit me all over again. My cousins thought it was hilarious; it was all a big joke to them. But to me, it was a nightmare come to life.

My fear of clowns began before I could talk. When I was just a toddler, my mom decorated my nursery in a circus theme, with clowns on a shelf whose heads turned when they laughed. One of my first words was "No!" as I pointed to those stupid clowns. Ever since I can remember, I've hated them.

My cousins, aunt, and uncle knew how much I hated clowns, and yet they saw it as an opportunity for entertainment at my expense—a harmless prank. I could see the glee in their eyes and hear the bursts of laughter. It hurt to realize that my fear—something very real and personal—was being used as a tool for ratings. I kept smiling for the cameras, wiping away sweat on my upper lip and trying to be a good sport, but inside I was embarrassed and furious, with questions swirling around in my mind and heart.

Do my feelings matter?

Do these people listen?

Do they care about me? Or am I just one big joke?

That episode of the show taught me a lot about boundaries and the importance of respecting other people's fears and vulnerabilities. It also revealed that the people who know us best can sometimes use that knowledge to be incredibly insensitive, even cruel.

Do you remember the "circle of trust" in the movie *Meet the Parents*? My family had their own version, but it was far more real and intimidating. Before filming began or late at night, my uncle Jim Bob would often call for a family meeting. I was never included in these meetings; instead, I was at times the topic of conversation. Two of my cousins once disclosed that Jim Bob would say things like, "Now, we don't have to tell Cousin Amy what we're talking about. We love her, but she doesn't follow our beliefs. We need to be careful not to let her influence the truth," or variations of that theme. This exclusion felt strange and hurtful because all I had ever been to my family was a safe place, a loving cousin who wanted to be part of their lives. But I think my uncle felt threatened that I might influence the kids to start thinking for themselves.

At some point, I stopped trying to please everyone and showed up to the filming session wearing a baseball hat and no makeup. I guess you could say my "give a dang" was busted. I was mentally drained and just didn't care anymore. What's really sad and heartbreaking is that once I made the decision to leave the show, I never had the chance to say goodbye to my cousins. One day I was there, and the next day I was just gone.

In what I could only interpret as an attempt to force me into silence, I was presented with an NDA (nondisclosure agreement) in 2019 by my uncle stating that if I left *Counting On*, I could never acknowledge my family publicly. I could never speak their names or discuss their family dynamics in any way.

But let me back up. Before I was handed the NDA, my uncle called and said, "Amy, I've been thinking about your time on the show and

I'd like to pay you something for your effort." I was really taken aback because he had never offered anything like that before.

"I'll have to think about it." And I did. A few days later, I called him back, and we began to discuss amounts.

"How much do you think you're worth?"

Pause. I had no idea how to answer such a question.

He jumped into the silence. "I mean, you chose to be a part of this ministry."

My brain raced, trying to come up with a number. "Well, I know the ratings skyrocketed, and a lot of episodes featured what I was doing on the show. So could we do one thousand dollars an episode?"

"I'm not paying that!" Since I was in so many episodes, I knew he'd quickly done the math and realized it wasn't a trivial amount.

"You were treated very well on the show," he said firmly. "We provided for you and we traveled. Gas in the RV is expensive, Amy. You didn't have to pay for any tickets to anything. And that number is absurd!"

I stuck to my number, so we went back and forth for a while. But I knew it was a losing battle. Here's what I wanted to say but didn't: "The *network* paid for the food, hotels, tickets, and gas and *you* still saw a hefty paycheck!"

Eventually, he offered me $10,000 for my time on the show. I was deeply frustrated but realized he wouldn't budge much. I was busy with a newborn baby at the time. I was a boutique owner and was ready to move on with my life. Still, I just couldn't believe his attitude. Finally, we settled on $30,000, and he brought a check to my store on a rainy afternoon. He also made my mom, Dillon, and me sign another NDA stating that we would never discuss the compensation. And that was the end of it. I believe it was "shut up" money because my uncle knew that Josh was being investigated for something more sinister than I could ever have fathomed.

After years of coming to peace with what had happened, my husband and I talked to several lawyers. We were told that an NDA like that would never hold up in court. What is in the public record cannot be legally denied, and I can't help the fact that my legal maiden name is, in fact, Duggar. I signed the first contract under false pretenses. They can't deny that I was on their reality show or that the Duggar family are my relatives. They most certainly cannot even come close to denying the heartbreaking public records about Josh and the scandals. We signed the NDA under false pretenses as well, not having been given all the necessary information. From my perspective, hidden motives and sneaky transactions were a pattern with my uncle.

My ties to my family were broken. One day I was included in our family group chat, and the next day I was deleted from it. Nobody would return my texts or phone calls. For years now, I have lived in fear and been kept in silence, scared that if I ever mentioned anything about my NDA, my uncle would come after me and I'd land in court.

I miss all my cousins terribly. It's not just one or two people I'm estranged from; I had to walk away from twenty people with whom I spent quality time almost daily. I held all of my cousins when they were born, shared inside jokes, and traveled with them. Each cousin had their own personality, and I enjoyed getting to know them as individuals, even if it was only on the surface. I've missed funerals and birthdays now—something I never thought I would do. I've been uninvited to weddings and reunions. I always brought treats for my cousins or at least a huge jar of pickles. I've spent a fortune on pickles through the years! Now it's so weird to think that if I tried to call my cousins, I would be ignored. My uncle controls who can contact them. There's no telling what he says about me—maybe, "She's always been jealous of you." Or, "Amy went down a dark path and isn't walking with Jesus, so you can't be around her." Or, "We just need to pray for Amy, Dillon, and Aunt Deanna."

The whole situation is so upsetting because I know they are most likely being fed lies. I can't do anything about it except to hope and pray that someday they will understand everything and that the truth will be revealed.

It's undeniable that my uncle has severe control issues. Those family meetings he called for at a moment's notice weren't just simple family meetings; they were orchestrated efforts to maintain control, to ensure that every member stayed aligned with the family's strict values and beliefs. The meetings were about reinforcing the rules, discussing behavior, and addressing potential threats to their way of life. And I, with my different views and Christian lifestyle, was seen as one of those threats.

Jim Bob's paranoia about my influence on his children was evident. He doesn't trust anyone who doesn't fit the mold. He emphasized the importance of staying away from my worldly ways, painting me as a potential corrupter of their pure and righteous path. I wasn't trying to lead anyone astray or impose my beliefs on them. I just wanted to be part of their lives, to share moments and memories with my cousins. But in their eyes, my lifestyle choices made me someone to be watched carefully and talked about behind closed doors. The family meetings were not just about control; they were about fear—fear of the unknown, fear of change, fear of seeing the rigid structure collapse that had been built over the years.

At one point, my uncle made up a new rule on the spot: "I think it's best for my children if you come over only when I'm there."

What? I've been coming to your house my whole life!

"I'd like you to call before you head over," he said firmly.

My mom thought his rule was ridiculous and the kids probably didn't even notice. I knew it was yet another way for him to assert control.

I wanted to be there for my cousins in every way possible to support them and love them unconditionally. But instead, Uncle Jim Bob made sure, in my opinion, that I was targeted as the black sheep, the one they were warned to stay away from for no worthy reason.

I loved my family deeply, and despite everything, I still do. But the pain of their rejection, the sting of being cast aside, will forever weigh on my heart. It's a wound that time can't seem to heal right now, a reminder of a bond that was broken. I often wonder if I could have done something different to prevent this heartache. Could I have played even a small part in saving us from this painful divide? The answer, like so many other instances in life, remains painfully out of reach. It's a deep, gnawing ache that never truly goes away, a constant reminder of the love I still have for them and the loss I feel every day.

One day not long after Grandma's funeral, my uncle was at our house with Mom and me. We were exhausted and heartbroken because the house felt so empty without Grandma. Suddenly Jim Bob spoke up. "Amy, have you heard from Jill lately?"

"I haven't." I wasn't sure why he was asking.

"She's really going through a lot," he said. "Something's not right with her."

"What do you think it is?" I asked.

"I don't know. I think she's surrounding herself with wrong friends and bad influences. Maybe you should reach out to her."

I still wasn't sure why he was asking me—probably another attempt at manipulation and control. But I loved my cousin, so I sent her a text message: **I'm here for you if you ever need to talk.**

A few days later I received the most unexpected text back from Jill: **Hey, cuz, where's a good tattoo parlor?**

I nearly fell out of my chair! I called her right away, and we couldn't stop laughing as she told me about the piercing she was planning to get.

After decades of smiling, hugging, and having only surface-level conversations, Jill and I have finally been able to connect on a deeper level. She opened up to me, and we both had so much to share. For the first time, I felt like I could truly be myself around one of my cousins. Now our kids are close; we shop together; I've watched her kids; Daxton goes to her house; and we have a normal, healthy cousinship that I'm deeply grateful for.

Sidenote: If you are a family member reading this book, I want you to know I love you and am so sorry for being forced out of your life. Please question everything you've been taught, so you can live in freedom. It breaks my heart to miss so much of your lives. I'm always here for you if you ever need me.

The truth matters. Standing up for it isn't just a choice for me; it's a responsibility, a vow I refuse to break because the truth is what stops the toxic cycle that holds generations in its grip. I've made my choice, and for the first time I feel true peace—not the fragile, conditional kind that comes from keeping up appearances, but the kind that comes from knowing I'm doing what's right. I no longer belong to anyone's side; I'm no longer bound by loyalty that demands silence over truth. I will not let deception, manipulation, and blind obedience shape my son's future the way it shaped my past. The cycle of delusion, fraud, and harm ends here.

TWENTY-ONE

Below Rock Bottom

Seven years had passed now. Life moved on—for most of my family at least. My cousins were celebrating milestones: new babies, weddings, graduations—all the markers of growing up and moving forward. On the surface, it seemed like the chaos was behind us, and those who had been hurt the most were finally finding solid ground again. There was a sense of renewed harmony in their smiles all over social media.

And honestly, I was genuinely happy for them. But I couldn't ignore the heavy feeling inside me—a sense that not all wounds had been fully healed or hurts properly faced. While everyone else appeared to be moving on, I kept my distance. My son has never spent time there—that boundary was set from the very beginning, and it's one I've never compromised. Many of my cousins never reached out, and I didn't reach out to most of them either. I simply focused on my marriage and building my own life.

More rumors were swirling about Josh, and we needed to know the truth. So one night, Dillon and I decided to call my uncle to get some answers. We hadn't spoken to him in a while, but we had heard new chatter about Josh and an odd visit that Homeland Security had made to a car lot where Josh worked.

We called Jim Bob and said, "Hey, listen, we're hearing some things about Homeland Security showing up at Josh's work. Please, if there's anything going on, we'd like to be told. The scandal blindsided us, and we don't want to be caught off guard again."

My uncle, ever the master of dismissing concerns, brushed it off. He said, "You know, being in the public eye is tough. People are always making up stories. I guess there wasn't much Hollywood news going on, so they needed something to talk about."

My heart dropped, and I felt sick. *What is going on?*

"Homeland Security only stopped by the car lot because one of their guys knows Josh and just wanted to stop in to say hello while they were in the area," my uncle continued. "There's no truth to anything the media is saying."

I wanted to believe him; I just wasn't sure I could anymore.

He reassured us, telling us that if anything serious developed, he would let us know. And of course, he asked us not to speak to the press because, "There's no reason to make it a big deal; they just stopped by."

We thanked him, and I told him how sorry I was for everything the family was going through. He was cordial, and we ended the call on a somewhat positive note.

But something about the conversation didn't sit right with me. Homeland Security doesn't just go for a casual drive and happen to pop into your business. Who was he kidding? I certainly wasn't buying the story he was selling. I told Dillon, "I can't shake the feeling that there's more to this." I'm not stupid or naive, but it sure felt like Uncle Jim Bob thought I was. I knew something wasn't adding up. I saw a report on the local news station about some ongoing investigation, and it was clear there had to be more to the story, like there always was. Even so, I decided not to probe anymore. I wanted to trust what Uncle Jim Bob had told us.

A few days later, after breastfeeding Dax and getting him to sleep, I decided to take a shower—something every mom knows provides a rare and precious moment of solitude. But soon after settling in to enjoy the steamy spray, my mom knocked frantically on the bathroom door, her voice shaky. "Amy," she said, "you need to come out right now. Some men are here to see you."

Confused and dripping wet, I quickly threw on some mismatched clothes and wrapped a towel around my head. I walked barefoot into the kitchen, and there, standing in front of me, were two men in black suits from Homeland Security.

"Are you Amy King?"

I nodded, my heart sinking. I couldn't believe what I was seeing and immediately felt overwhelmed. I invited them in, and we sat on the couch while my mom checked on Dax in the nursery.

Though the men couldn't share specific details, they told me that additional discoveries showed that Josh's actions were very serious, far worse than what the media had already reported.

I felt my stomach plummet in shock, tears welling up in my eyes as they spoke.

They asked me about the computer—the one I had told Uncle Jim Bob about years ago that had "Josh's Files" on it. Jill had told the agents about the computer and the disturbing photos and videos, and now they were coming to ask me if I had seen anything suspicious on Josh's computer.

I couldn't believe the questions they were asking me, questions about whether I saw any pictures in Josh's files that contained children. I sat there in disbelief, my mind racing back to that time. I told them I hadn't seen any images of children, but to be honest, I didn't see a lot. The few images I had seen were enough to make me sick to my stomach, and I couldn't bear to look further. Here I was years later, being asked about those same files, realizing that it was all far worse than I had imagined.

Josh had texted me just a couple of weeks earlier, acting as if everything was normal. Now, learning of this new horrible truth, I was devastated. My cousin, whom I had grown up with, played with, and laughed with, had been leading a vile secret life. Not only had he engaged in incest and adultery, but he had immersed himself in the most despicable behavior toward innocent children.

After the Homeland Security agents left, I cried for days. My face became inflamed. I couldn't sleep. It was all too awful to process. I felt sick to my stomach again, far worse than when I'd seen those images on his computer.

But in those few moments with the investigators, the truth became undeniable. Josh had made a series of horrifically costly decisions and now he was justly facing severe legal consequences.

Uncle Jim Bob had lied to us. Again. He had known all along why Homeland Security stopped to see his son that day, and he had done everything he could to keep us and everyone else in the dark. It wasn't about protecting me or the family; it was about protecting their precious image. We were just collateral damage in this twisted game. Now the consequences of that deception were unfolding before me, more painful and devastating than I ever could have anticipated.

And it wasn't just one lie. During the investigation Uncle Jim Bob told us a whole host of lies:

Lie #1: An ex-con worked at the Duggar car lot, and he was the one being investigated, not Josh.

Lie #2: Josh was not working that day.

Lie #3: Josh's friend who worked at Homeland Security had
stopped by the car lot for a quick visit to say hi.

Lie #4: Homeland Security was checking out several local
businesses; this was just a routine check to make sure
everything was operating correctly in the northwest
Arkansas community.

Lie #5: The media was lying and just randomly picked our family
for a juicy story.

Lie #6: The media likes to portray the Duggar family in a poor
light because we stand up for what is right.

Lie #7: The media is secular, and its reporters don't know Jesus;
therefore they attack Christians.

Lie #8: Homeland Security couldn't find the address they
were supposed to go to, so they stopped by the car lot for
directions.

Lie #9: Local government leaders who didn't agree with the
Duggar lifestyle were upset and were attacking our family.

Lie #10: Joseph Biden was president, not Donald Trump, so that's
why Josh was being investigated over some legal matters.

Can we all laugh together at that last one?

Out of the blue, the entire Duggar clan, including Josh and Anna, came to my house one day. Josh held my newborn son for hours. At the time, I knew nothing about the ongoing investigation that would later prove that Josh was a child sex offender. This was a new level of disrespect and betrayal that hurt me to my core, that he came and chose to hold my son, as if nothing had happened. If I had known then what I know now, I would never have allowed any of the Duggars into my home with my newborn.

People who lie to you cannot be taken at face value because their words and actions are built on deception. When someone repeatedly bends the truth, hides information, or manipulates facts, it becomes impossible to trust what they say. It's exhausting to second-guess someone constantly. Their words become meaningless, and their actions are the only thing left to measure.

> People who lie to you cannot be taken at face value because their words and actions are built on deception.

Maybe the truth was too painful to bear, and the weight of it more than Uncle Jim Bob could handle. So he let the lies start small, and with each denial, each cover-up, the little snowball of dishonesty grew into a massive snow roller until it was impossible to stop. Oh, the irony of how big that snowball became! Maybe deception felt safer than facing the wreckage that honesty would bring. But no matter how carefully he packed layer upon layer of falsehoods, no matter how many times he convinced himself—or others—that everything was fine, the truth was never far behind, waiting for the moment when the weight of all the lies would finally cause his world to come crashing down around him. And in the end, no matter how desperately he tried to outrun the truth, it caught up to him. It always does.

In April 2021, my cousin Josh was arrested by federal agents on charges of receiving and possessing child sexual abuse material (CSAM).

November 2021: The trial began on November 30, 2021, in Fayetteville, Arkansas. Federal prosecutors presented evidence that Josh had downloaded explicit material involving children as young as eighteen months old. Computer forensics experts testified that he had installed a Linux partition on his work computer to bypass accountability software and access the dark web, where he downloaded the illegal content in May 2019.

A key element of the prosecution's case centered on digital evidence that linked Josh to the material. The defense suggested that someone else could have remotely accessed his computer or been physically present to download the files, but this argument failed to convince the jury.

After seven hours of deliberation, on December 9, 2021, the jury unanimously found Josh guilty on both counts. During the sentencing phase, Judge Timothy L. Brooks called the material "the sickest of the sick" and noted Josh's lack of responsibility or remorse.

On May 25, 2022, Josh was sentenced to 151 months (12 years and 7 months) in federal prison, followed by twenty years of supervised release under strict conditions, including no unsupervised contact with minors, mandatory therapy, and restrictions on internet usage. He was transferred to the Federal Correctional Institute (FCI) Seagoville in Texas to serve his sentence.[10]

Josh had clearly been leading a sad, sickening double life for a very long time. The first two scandals were awful; this third scandal was horrifying, as low and dark as one could go. There's nothing more heartbreaking than children being abused, and the fact that he downloaded this evil material showed just how far he had fallen.

As I looked back on our conversations with Jim Bob before Josh was arrested and tried, it was clear that Dillon, Daxton, my mom, and I meant nothing to my uncle. He didn't care about our well-being, nor did he think we deserved his honesty. To see someone who should represent support, trust, and family be so heartless and calculating was disheartening beyond words.

The truth is, there's no room for excuses anymore. We all know people who can talk the talk—quote Scripture, look the part—but how often do we stop to question whether their actions match their words? Just because someone appears to have all the right answers doesn't mean they're beyond reproach. Even Satan can quote Scripture (Matthew 4:6), but that doesn't make him righteous. So why do we so easily let people hide behind a facade of faith when their actions tell a completely different story?

We've all been there—confused by someone who appears to be a faultless example of faith and virtue, but then when we take a closer look, we realize something is off. Maybe it's a family member, a church leader, or even a close friend who says all the right things but never genuinely backs them up. What do we do when we see this disconnect? Do we ignore the red flags because it's easier than confronting the truth? Do we keep letting them off the hook because we've been taught to trust them, to give them the benefit of the doubt?

How often have you let someone slide because of their position, their words, or their reputation? How many times have you stayed silent, thinking it's not your place to say something? Or refused to confront someone because they are family and we love them and we don't want to ruffle any feathers?

It's not easy, to be sure, but standing up for the truth will sometimes mean calling out the things that don't make sense. Real faith is about more than just words; it's about living out the truth consistently. No matter who's watching or what title they have—boss, neighbor, friend, spouse, family member, or even someone in your church—it's all about your character.

> Real faith is about more than just words; it's about living out the truth consistently, no matter who's watching.

This darkness—the denial, the secrecy, the silence—falls on my uncle. It falls on my grandpa. It even falls on my great-grandpa. But here's the thing: It doesn't have to continue. It will *not* fall on me. Generational curses, those chains of dysfunction and pain that have bound my family for so long, must be broken. I'm committed to breaking them for the sake of my own family and for future generations. I refuse to let that darkness pass down any further.

I don't hate my family members, even the ones who have boldly lied to me. As hard as it has been, I do forgive my uncle for his lies, even though he has never asked for forgiveness. But a snake in the grass is still a snake. Forgiveness doesn't mean I have to let this kind of deceit or manipulation back into my life. I consider Uncle Jim Bob's deceit a character flaw, and therefore I don't consider him a safe person. I've learned the hard way that just because we forgive someone doesn't mean we need to welcome them with open arms. Trust is earned, and broken trust cannot be easily restored.

Trust is the foundation of any genuine relationship. Without it, what do we really have? Words become empty, love feels conditional, and every interaction carries an undercurrent of doubt. Trust is more than just believing what someone says; it's knowing their actions will align with their words. It's about feeling safe emotionally and physically in their presence. When trust is broken, it fractures everything, leaving behind a version of love that is more about obligation than connection. And when we can't trust our own family members, the betrayal cuts even deeper.

I truly feel sorry for my cousins. I've watched them grow up in an environment where manipulation, secrecy, and control are the norm. The parenting

> Trust is more than just believing what someone says; it's knowing their actions will align with their words. It's about feeling safe emotionally and physically in their presence.

they've experienced has left them trapped in a pattern of pretending that everything's perfect while hiding the ugly truth. I understand their love and respect for their parents, which, sadly, is entangled in a web of obedience and submission required for them to belong.

I can only imagine the confusion my cousins must feel, being caught between what they've been taught and what they've witnessed. They've been raised to defend the lies because that's all they've ever known. It breaks my heart to think of how much they've missed out on—genuine unconditional love, the kind where we can be ourselves without fear of being judged or manipulated. I wish they could see the world differently, but I know they're deeply rooted in what they've been taught and it's not easy to walk away from it.

My son will grow up in a home where truth is not twisted to fit an agenda, where love is not a tool for control, and where faith is lived out with sincerity, not just performed to gain the approval of others. I will do whatever it takes to ensure he knows the difference between real faith and an empty facade. In the end, what we pass down to our children isn't just our stated beliefs; it's also the way we live out those beliefs day after day.

I've seen firsthand how patterns of abuse, secrecy, and neglect can completely destroy lives. I've watched it tear apart my family. I will not be the one who turns a blind eye anymore or sweeps things under the rug in order to keep up appearances. I will confront the truth head-on, no matter how uncomfortable, no matter how painful. That's the only way real healing happens. It's the only way to stop the cycle from repeating itself. It is the way of a holy disruptor.

TWENTY-TWO

Rest in the Storm

Writing down my story has been one of the most challenging things I've ever done. I've been pushed to the limit, forced to confront parts of myself and my past that I prefer to leave buried. As I began to dig deeper, feelings and memories surfaced—some so painful that I had hidden them away for years, hoping I'd never have to revisit them. I convinced myself that by burying those experiences, I was protecting myself from further hurt. But in reality, I was carrying a weight that was crushing me.

The writing process has been painful but also transformative. For the first time, I am able to look at my life honestly, without shoving things into the dark corners of my mind. In giving my story a voice, I could finally release some of the pain I had been carrying in silence. It's shown me that while trauma may have left its mark, it doesn't have to define my future. I've experienced many moments when fear crept in, leaving me questioning whether I was strong enough to keep going.

I've doubted myself more times than I can count and care to admit. Never in a million years could I have imagined I'd be a cast member of a reality show, estranged from my family, or writing a memoir. For so many years, I carried everything inside—pain, confusion, and years of silence stretching all the way back to my childhood.

But now as I look back, I realize how much baggage I was carrying without even knowing it, and how thoroughly I was denying myself a chance to heal. I never imagined finding myself in a place where I could speak openly, let alone share my story in a way that would bring understanding and growth. I used to see myself as anything but bold, as someone who shied away from confrontation at all costs. But now I can't keep ignoring all that has been so wrong. I've come to understand that silence doesn't heal; it just prolongs the hurt. Embracing the truth, no matter how difficult or painful, is the only path forward.

It's easy to justify dysfunction when it's all we've ever known. We tell ourselves, *That's just how they are. It's not that bad. All families fight, right?* But there's a difference between normal disagreements and patterns of manipulation, control, and emotional neglect. When love comes with conditions—when we're accepted only as long as we comply—that's not love; that's control.

> When love comes with conditions—when we're accepted only as long as we comply—that's not love; that's control.

Anyone who treats you abusively does not love you, plain and simple. Love is built on respect, kindness, and mutual care—not control, manipulation, or emotional blackmail. So when someone keeps violating your boundaries or makes you question reality through mind games, that's not love; it's control. And you absolutely have the right to walk away from that nonsense, even if it means cutting ties with people you thought would always be in your life. Because honestly, staying around just to keep the peace? Not worth losing your sanity over.

If you're seeking healing from narcissistic abuse, let me gently remind you to give yourself grace—more grace than you think you need. Healing is not a straightforward journey, and triggers can surface when you least expect them. One day you may feel strong and in control; the next day something that seems small can send you into a wave of anxiety or fear.

This happened to me recently as I was driving behind a truck hauling wood-chipping machinery. Out of nowhere, my hands grew clammy, my heart raced, and fear washed over me for a split second. It was confusing at first, but then I realized that my body was reacting to an old memory—something painful from my past—and this object had stirred it up.

Triggers often operate in a hidden space, bringing back memories or feelings from a time when we felt vulnerable or unsafe. They can come from anything—a sound, a smell, a word—and suddenly we're transported back to a moment when we were deeply hurt. It might be the smell of a certain cologne, a tone of voice, or even a phrase like "we need to talk," which, in the past, signaled conflict or manipulation. When those moments come, our minds may feel overwhelmed, and we may question why we feel this way.

But remember this: You're not alone in this experience. It's important to understand that triggers aren't always logical. Your rational mind may know you're in a safe place, but your emotional mind—still healing from past wounds—sends out alarms as though you're still in danger. Your body holds on to those memories of fear, even when you've worked hard to heal. And when these memories are stirred up, it's not a sign of failure; it's just part of the journey.

The key is to give yourself permission to feel whatever emotions arise. Let the fear, sadness, or anxiety rise. You are no longer in that difficult place, and the person or situation that hurt you doesn't have control over you anymore. You're in control now. Slowly, with time and practice, you can regain your sense of peace in these moments. It's a process, but one that you can navigate with compassion for yourself.

Triggers don't define your progress; they're simply echoes of the past. With each passing day, you are growing stronger, and the more you acknowledge and work through these moments, the more peace you will experience. You've come this far, and you deserve every bit of grace and compassion along the way. You are stronger than the fear, stronger than the memories. You have the ability to reclaim your peace.

> You have the ability to reclaim your peace.

Emotional abuse can be difficult to recognize because it often operates under the surface, slowly eroding your sense of self and warping your perception of reality. It's not always as obvious as physical violence, but its effects are just as damaging, leaving long-lasting wounds that can be difficult to heal from. Understanding the various forms of emotional abuse and tactics is crucial in breaking free from their grip. Let me walk you through some examples of what emotional abuse looks like in everyday life (many of which are from my own experiences). It's time to reevaluate who you allow to stay close to you if they exhibit any of these toxic behaviors:

- lying or distorting the truth
- blaming and criticizing you constantly, even for things that aren't your fault
- manipulating situations to make themselves look better or you feel small
- overreacting or creating unnecessary drama
- operating unfairly or playing favorites

- refusing to apologize or offering shallow, insincere apologies
- lacking genuine concern or interest in your well-being or your life
- having volatile moods and unpredictable behavior that keep you on edge
- making cruel, critical remarks that are relentless and unprovoked
- showing favoritism to others
- ignoring your feelings
- refusing to take responsibility for their behavior
- passing judgment on you
- creating so much stress, anxiety, and pain that your health, ability to work, or general well-being are negatively impacted
- interacting with you in a way makes you feel worse
- giving the feeling that they are always right (and you are always wrong)

Emotional abuse, manipulation, and toxic behavior are never acceptable, no matter where they come from. You do not have to tolerate those behaviors. It may feel like you're betraying someone or breaking an unwritten rule about loyalty to family, but letting go doesn't make you cold or heartless; it makes you brave. You deserve a life of peace, filled with people who genuinely care for you. Protecting that peace is your right. Even if that someone who is abusing you happens to be a family member, it doesn't give anyone permission to harm you. Choosing yourself isn't selfish; it's survival.

One of the most insidious forms of emotional abuse is **gaslighting**, which refers to another person's practice of denying facts or twisting the truth until we question our own memory and even our sanity. We begin to doubt our grasp of reality and our perceptions. My dad was a master at this. After our counseling session together, there came a time when I questioned whether we had actually gone to counseling together or I had just dreamed it up. He was so convincing in his denial that I almost believed him. He constantly made me feel like I was overreacting or imagining things. Gaslighting leaves a person feeling lost, disoriented, and unsure of their own mind, making it easier for the abuser to maintain control.

Manipulation is another common tactic. Abusers use charm, lies, and deceit to get what they want, often preying on our emotions and vulnerabilities. In my case, poems were weaponized against me. Something that should have been a form of expression and connection was twisted into a tool for manipulation, making me feel guilty or inadequate if I failed to respond in the way my dad expected. Manipulation can be subtle or over-the-top, but it always involves using our feelings against us to serve someone else's agenda.

Isolation is a powerful tool in the emotional abuser's arsenal. They cut us off from friends, family, and other support systems, making us more dependent on them. This doesn't always happen overnight—it's gradual. We may stop reaching out to friends because the abuser makes us feel guilty for spending time away from them or criticizes our relationships. Before we know it, we're alone, compelled to rely entirely on the person causing us harm. This isolation allows them to control the narrative and limit our ability to seek help or validation from others. I felt completely isolated in my pain and I felt like no one would understand or care.

Then there's **emotional abuse** in its most straightforward form—belittling, shaming, and criticizing us in ways that slowly chip away at our self-esteem. My dad would constantly criticize me. He made me feel hugely insecure to the point where I could focus only on negative qualities about myself.

Abusers also exert **control and domination** over our lives. They micromanage our choices, our actions, and sometimes even our thoughts, dictating what we should think, feel, or do. This control can be extreme, like telling us what to wear or where we can go, or it can be subtle, like making us feel guilty for making decisions on our own. It's about maintaining power and keeping us dependent on their approval. I wasn't allowed to make certain decisions without fear of a passive-aggressive comment or a full-blown outburst. The constant need to avoid conflict left me feeling like I had no control over my own life.

Projection is another common tactic in emotional abuse. The abuser will accuse us of their own faults, turning the tables so we're the ones who feel guilty or at fault. It's a mind-bending form of abuse because it leaves us feeling like we're the problem when, in reality, they're projecting their own flaws onto us.

One of the most painful tactics is **triangulation**, where the abuser involves others in conflicts to create drama and confusion. They pit people against each other, often making them feel isolated and unsupported. My dad would talk to my mom about me behind my back, creating a web of confusion and mistrust. This made it difficult to know who to turn to, as everyone seemed to be involved in some version of the story that wasn't true.

Then there's **love bombing**, where the abuser overwhelms us with affection and attention, only to later withdraw it. It's a manipulation technique designed to gain our trust and make us emotionally dependent on them. At first, it feels like love—intense, passionate, and all-consuming—but once they have us hooked, they pull away, leaving us desperate for their affection to return. It's a cruel pattern that keeps us trapped in a relationship, always hoping for the return of the good times.

The **silent treatment** is another form of emotional abuse, where the abuser uses silence as a weapon. They withdraw communication as a form of punishment, leaving us in a state of anxiety and confusion. It's a way to make us feel small and insignificant, as if our presence doesn't even warrant a response. This tactic keeps us on edge, always waiting for the moment they decide to acknowledge us again. There were times when I felt like a ghost within the walls of our house, like when I'd ask my dad a question and he wouldn't acknowledge me.

Intimidation and threats also play a significant role in emotional abuse. These can be direct or implied, but the goal is always the same—to keep us in line through fear. Threats of harm, abandonment, or other consequences loom large over every interaction. I remember constantly fearing the next outburst or emotional ambush. It was like living with a ticking time bomb, never knowing when it would go off.

Another hallmark of emotional abuse is **lies and deception**. The abuser frequently lies or omits truths to maintain control and manipulate our perception. We start questioning what's real and what's not, which only deepens the abuser's hold over us. They create a world where they control the narrative, making it impossible for us to discern the truth.

In some cases, emotional abuse takes the form of **financial control**. Even as adults, we may find ourselves financially dependent on the abuser, who restricts our access to money or makes us feel guilty for spending anything. This keeps us trapped in the relationship, unable to break free because we don't have the resources to support ourselves.

The abuser may also engage in **exploitation**, taking advantage of our time, energy, and resources for their own benefit. They demand everything from us but offer nothing in return, which leaves us feeling drained and unappreciated, as if our needs don't matter.

One of the most frustrating tactics is **blame shifting**. The abuser refuses to take responsibility for their actions, always finding a way to make us or someone else the scapegoat. No matter the situation, they are never at fault. This constant shifting of blame leaves us feeling confused and powerless, as if no matter what we do, we'll always be in the wrong.

Sometimes, abusers recruit **flying monkeys** to reinforce their narrative. They gather allies who help them spread their version of events, making us feel outnumbered and isolated. It can feel like the whole world is against us, and that's exactly what the abuser wants. I experienced a swarm of flying monkeys calling me when I decided to cut ties with my dad.

Withholding affection is a deeply painful weapon wielded by abusers. They use love and affection as a tool, giving and taking it away to control our emotions and behavior. It's conditional love. I know this tactic far too well. My dad often refused to hug me unless I did something to earn that love. For example, I'd have to rake the leaves or make his favorite meal before he'd offer any love. I never felt like he hugged me because he actually loved me.

I was in my late twenties when I started to see things for what they truly were. I began to understand that the constant fear and tension we lived with wasn't normal, that not everyone grew up with the threat of angry outbursts occurring at any moment. I realized that home wasn't supposed to feel like a battlefield. The more I looked at my father's behavior, the more I saw the patterns. His moments of intense affection—the love bombs—followed by periods of coldness and cruelty were all part of a manipulative Ferris wheel designed to keep my mom and me going around and around with no stop in sight.

The truth is, we can't make someone love us, and we certainly can't change someone who doesn't want to change. If my mom had gotten the healing she needed from her father, maybe she would have seen that she deserved so much more than what my dad did to her.

Maybe she would have realized that love is not about living in fear. Love is not abuse. And while I believe that God has a plan for each of us, no matter the suffering we endure, I still wish she could have been spared from such intense heartache.

My dad, in his own brokenness, repeated the same cycle of hatred and emotional abuse that he had experienced as a child. He became the very thing that hurt him, passing down the pain from one generation to the next. How tragic is it to know that things could have been different, that the cycle could have ended with him if he had just acknowledged his own wounds and sought healing.

I can see now how deeply all of this affected me. Growing up in such an unstable, volatile environment shaped everything about me—my relationships, my sense of self-worth, even my movement through the world. For more than twenty years, I walked on eggshells, constantly trying to avoid conflict, constantly trying to keep the peace. I became a master at people-pleasing, doing everything I could to avoid rocking the boat.

It took years—years of unlearning those patterns of panic and self-doubt—before I could begin to rebuild a sense of safety within myself. I had to learn how to recognize my triggers, how to stop waiting for the other shoe to drop, and how to create a sense of peace and stability in my life. Because the truth is, security isn't just about having a roof over your head or food on the table; it's about feeling safe—emotionally, mentally, and physically. It's the foundation on which everything else in your life is built. And when you grow up without that sense of security, you're constantly scrambling to find your footing, trying to build something stable in the midst of chaos.

I don't hate my dad. In fact, I have compassion for him. It's hard to hold on to anger when I see the pain and trauma he has carried with him all these years. And although I don't know the full story of what he's been through, I know enough to understand that he's not free. As much as I wish my dad could have found healing, I know now that I can't save him. The journey to healing is one that only he can take, and sadly, he's never chosen it. But I pray that he will be delivered and that I can protect my child from ever having to experience the kind of pain that was passed down to me.

I refuse to let the cycle repeat itself. I've chosen a different path, one that breaks the chains of abuse. My dad may be in bondage, but I'm not. I chose to work through my trauma to be as healthy as I can for those I love.

As we fight for our own healing, we must also protect our children's well-being in every way possible. They're too young to grasp the deep scars that abuse can leave, too innocent to bear such a burden. We are their voice, their shield, and their safe place, and I will never compromise on that commitment to my son. Because if we want to leave a legacy of strength and love, we must begin with our dedication to be whole—for ourselves and for them. I couldn't stop the emotional abuse growing up, but I can give Daxton a beautiful childhood. I will teach him what abuse is and warn him about the dangers of this world. I will protect my child from any experience of abuse, and I will be careful to guard who has access to him. Forgiving my father was a step toward freedom. Protecting my child is the ultimate act of love. My father will never have the opportunity to hurt my son the way he hurt me. That's a boundary I will never compromise.

When I was young, I used to think peace meant silence—no yelling, no arguing, no uneasy glances exchanged across a crowded room. But as I grew up, I discovered that peace is so much more. True peace is a state of the heart that remains steady, even when life tries to rattle us. I craved true peace more than anything. But after years of healing and therapy and working through obstacles, I've learned how to regain control over my emotions. I've worked hard to develop a sense of awareness, to catch myself before I spiral. Now when something triggers me, instead of letting it fester, I stop it in its tracks. I've learned to say, "Hey, what you're saying or doing is really triggering me, and I need you to stop."

It sounds simple, but for me, it's revolutionary. I've learned to acknowledge the pain in the moment rather than suppress it or let it explode out of me later. The difference now is that I deal with the hurt before it becomes a toxin that seeps into my relationships. I no longer let the pain of my past define how I interact with the people I love. I've realized that while I can't control what happened to me, I can control how I respond to it now. My son will not grow up carrying the same emotional weight I did.

Peace, I've learned, is like a light. When you have it, it shines, no matter how dark everything around you may be. Here's the thing I've realized: Peace is more than just a feeling; peace is a person—Jesus. He doesn't offer peace as a temporary distraction or a surface-level escape. He embodies it. When Jesus steps into our lives, he doesn't just give us a fleeting sense of calm; he brings a profound, lasting peace that nothing else can match.

One of my favorite reminders of this peace is found in the story narrated in Mark 4:35–41. Jesus and his disciples are in a boat, crossing the Sea of Galilee. A furious storm suddenly whips up out of nowhere. Waves are crashing over the boat, the winds are howling, and the whole boat is being tossed around like a toy. The disciples—who are seasoned fishermen, mind you—are terrified, convinced they're about to die. And Jesus? He's in the back of the boat, *asleep*. Completely undisturbed by the loud claps of thunder and the shouts and prayers of the men who were scared for their life.

The disciples finally snap. Dripping wet, cold, and angry, they rush over to Jesus and shake him awake. "Teacher, don't you care if we drown?" (Mark 4:38). They're panicking, and here's Jesus—completely unbothered. Jesus doesn't scramble to address the situation or join them in their panic. He simply stands up, maybe stretches a little, and speaks to the howling wind and the raging waves: "Peace, be still" (v. 39 KJV). And just like that, the wind and the sea obey him. The wind stops blowing; the waves disappear. Sudden and glorious peace.

I imagine the disciples standing there in stunned silence, their hearts still pounding, while everything around them is perfectly calm. Jesus turns to them and asks, "Why are you so afraid? Do you still have no faith?" (v. 40). It's like he's saying, "Don't you get it? I am with you, and when I'm here, you're safe, no matter what kind of storm is raging all around you."

I once had the dream of being a storm chaser. Storms have long held a fascination and appeal for me. The way storms are beyond our control, along with their power and intensity, has always drawn me in. But no storm is more powerful than Jesus.

That scene has become a powerful life lesson for me. The truth is, we all go through storms—moments when life feels out of control and we think, *This is it; I'm going under.* And in those moments, we often panic and toss and turn at night. We freak out or lash out at others and forget that we have Jesus right there with us. Jesus isn't panicking. He isn't worried. He's there, ready to calm the storm when the time is right. His peace isn't affected by the waves engulfing us.

But here's something interesting: Why doesn't Jesus just calm the storm before it gets started? Why wait until his disciples are at their wit's end? God sometimes lets the storm rage a little longer than we'd like, not because he's ignoring us, but because he's teaching us something deeper. He's using the storm to build trust in us, draw us closer to him, and teach us to stay calm, even when things get unbearable in our lives.

It's easy to trust God when everything is going smoothly, but true peace comes from learning to lean on God in the storm. We want quick fixes, but Jesus is often more interested in deepening our faith and anchoring our hearts. He doesn't just want to calm the storm *around* us; he wants to calm the storm *inside* us.

> He doesn't just want to calm the storm *around* us; he wants to calm the storm *inside* us.

Let's get real for a minute. The storms of life are everywhere. Whether they are personal struggles, financial challenges, difficult relationships, or the weight of the world's problems, we all face things that threaten to rob us of our peace every single day. Look at the world today. The news is filled with stories of tragedy, division, and heartbreak. It all feels so overwhelming. Every day, things seem to be getting progressively worse. But here's the truth: Just because the world is in chaos doesn't mean your heart has to be.

Filtering everything through the lens of peace has brought a new clarity to my life. My focus will be on creating space for what truly brings me joy, growth, and rest.

When the disciples woke Jesus up during the storm, it wasn't because they needed more strength to row the boat or a better strategy to ensure their survival. They needed peace. And when Jesus spoke, peace came not just to the storm but to their hearts as well.

It's important to remember that God doesn't promise a storm-free life. Let go of all your desire to control and say, *God, I can't do this anymore without you.* In that moment of surrender, his peace will wash over you, the kind of peace that transcends all understanding (Philippians 4:7).

The storms of life are inevitable. When the bills pile up, when your relationships are strained, when the baby keeps you up all night long, when your spouse is aloof and distant, when someone you trust lies to you, when you don't think real love exists, when you're pulling your hair out because of your kids and you're overwhelmed with worry—bring it all to the foot of the cross.

I've made it a priority to step back and assess every person, place, and thing in my life as I hold it up to one simple but powerful question:

"Does this bring me peace?" The Bible reminds us, "God is not a God of disorder but of peace" (1 Corinthians 14:33). So if something brings disorder, chaos, confusion, or drama into our lives, I know it's not aligned with God's will for me. His desire is for us to live in peace, with clarity of mind, heart, and purpose. That peace allows us to hear his voice more clearly, to navigate life with wisdom, and to make decisions that align with his plan for us.

I no longer feel pressured to stand up for myself just to be liked, accepted, or understood. I'm finally comfortable simply being me, without needing approval or validation. If that's not enough for some people, I'm at peace with that. I've let go of the need to make everyone happy or to avoid conflict by walking on eggshells. The person God made me to be is enough. I am already loved beyond measure, and I don't have anything to prove. This journey toward peace has shown me the beauty of living authentically—free, grounded, and at rest that I am exactly who I am meant to be.

I am safe in God's presence. So are you. In moments when the fear of the unknown feels overwhelming, I hold on to God's promise that I am never alone. His presence is the one constant in my life, even in the midst of doubt and uncertainty. I feel his Spirit within me, giving me the strength to keep moving forward, one step at a time. It's his power that fuels my courage to open up, bare my soul, and share my story in all its raw, unfiltered truth.

As you read these words, I hope they will be a light on your own path, helping you connect the dots. Maybe they'll encourage you to share your own story or take the first steps toward healing. When it feels like what you're facing is too much to bear, let God's presence give you courage. Let his promises lift you when it feels unspeakably hard to keep going. With each deep breath, remind yourself of this: You are capable, you are resilient, and you are held by a love that knows no limits.

TWENTY-THREE

"Peace, Be Still"

A special kind of peace comes from intentionally choosing a different path than the one you were shown. I'm learning that it's okay to reinvent my life. A big part of that for me is motherhood. Being a mom offers an opportunity to break cycles and redefine what love, respect, and discipline look like. One example is how I'm reimagining homeschooling. When I was growing up, I saw my cousins sitting at their desks, flipping through textbooks, and following a rigid schedule that looked like anything but fun. When I decided I wanted to homeschool Dax, I knew there had to be another way. So I set out to create a homeschooling experience that felt alive, exciting, and tailored to what my child needs most.

In our home, homeschooling means stomping in mud puddles, learning about rock formations by exploring nature trails, and diving into history by visiting museums. Recess? It's a bike ride around the neighborhood, a game of tag in the backyard, or a summer picnic with flash cards and Dax's favorite books spread out under a shady tree. I want Daxton to discover the beauty of curiosity—to light up at the sight of a cool-looking bug or find joy in the process of learning something new by playing fun games. We fill our days with cooking lessons, cleaning tips, and money management instruction. Let's face it, these are the life skills schools often fail to teach.

Our days are overflowing with laughter, playdates, and as much joy as we can pack in. Daxton's a social butterfly like his dad, but he has a quiet side too, like me. He loves being around people but needs time to recharge. That's okay because our version of homeschool lets him thrive at his own pace. While traditional homeschooling may have a reputation for being dull, in our household it's an explosion of creativity, hands-on experiences, and meaningful moments. Alongside homeschooling is another cornerstone of our home—gentle parenting. Dillon and I have chosen to approach parenting with communication instead of with a heavy hand or, worse, a belt. Daxton is growing up in a household built on respect rather than fear. When boundaries are tested (and let's be real, kids will always test boundaries), we don't resort to punishing, yelling, or shaming. Instead, we focus on understanding. We aim to communicate with a loving tone and with a view to correcting behavior.

When Daxton is having a hard time, I'll say, "Hey, buddy, let's take a little rest." Sometimes we all need to reset, and that's okay. When I need his attention, I'll say, "Eyes on me," and he knows to pause and focus. This kind of connection teaches him that his feelings are valid and that we're here to guide, not control. It's a work in progress for all of us, but it's worth it all to see him growing into a confident, loving little boy.

A tidy home is important to me, so after Daxton and I make a mess, we have cleanup time together. It's a way to teach responsibility and teamwork. I want Dillon to come home to order and a clean house with dinner ready. I'm traditional like that, and I love creating a space that feels warm and inviting for my family.

Dillon, though, is the type of husband who won't let me carry the load alone. He's an incredible cook—his brunches are top-notch, and I love the times he grills steak for dinner. On special nights, he'll draw me a bubble bath, complete with a tray of chocolates and a glass of wine. He's attentive and caring in ways that remind me daily of how blessed I am to have him by my side. Together, we've built a life filled with mutual respect, support, and deep love. To be sure, we've had our challenges, just like every couple does, but after ten years of being together, we still choose each other every day.

Having my mom live with us means more to me than words can express. She is safe now and finding peace too. For so long, my heart was weighed down with so much pain, but now it feels like my inner child is finally healing. It's as though God is restoring the years that were stolen from us, giving us this precious time to be together. We do everything together, and it's everything I've ever wanted.

My mom has been through so much, and every moment with her feels so special. Dax loves surprising his Nana with flowers. She absolutely adores surprises, so we're always finding new ways to show her how deeply loved she is. We go on random shopping trips, complete with a big scoop of ice cream at the end of the day. She has even started loving thrifting with me! We share relaxing spa days together at home while Dillon and Dax go to his family's farm. There's just this beautiful life we have created—one that could only have come from disrupting the toxic cycles. No more yelling, no more chaos and no more fear—but instead, there are simple, slow, beautiful days. My life now is a powerful answer to prayer. Deep down, I always knew things could be different. I fought hard to build the life we have today, making difficult choices that ultimately paved the way for the beauty we now live in as the King family + Nana.

Seeing the way Mom bonds with Daxton brings me indescribable joy. The two of them have the best time together—always laughing, creating silly songs, and coming up with fun games. Their laughter fills our home, and it's the sweetest sound. Watching them enjoy each other so much feels like a gift I didn't know I needed. She has become such a huge help to our family in ways I never imagined. Whether it's her wisdom, her presence, or her constant support, having her in my corner is a blessing I will never take for granted. To have her living with us isn't just about proximity; it's about redemption, healing, and love. It's a beautiful reminder that God can take the broken pieces of our lives and turn them into something much more beautiful than we ever imagined.

Peace, for me, looks like opening a window and letting the sunlight in. Now when I do, I don't see clutter or chaos; I see clarity. The air is light and fresh. I can breathe freely. I'm no longer tiptoeing through tension or walking on eggshells. I'm no longer in survival mode. I grew up surrounded by constant yelling, and now my days are filled with serenity. It's one of the most incredible gifts I've ever received!

As a little girl, I used to whisper to myself, *It won't always be like this*. And now—it isn't. I've learned that family isn't just blood; it's love, loyalty, and choice. DNA doesn't grant automatic access to my life. The truth is, friends can become family, and chosen family can be the most healing kind.

There are moments when I just stop and take it all in—a simple movie night, Daxton curled up between us, our favorite snacks within reach, and Dillon's arm wrapped around me. There's a quiet, easy calm, something I never really knew before. And in those small, ordinary moments of being a family, I feel it—pure happiness. I can't put it into words, but deep down I know this is the life I once only dreamed of having.

There was a time when my mother and I carried so much pain

between us that even a simple embrace felt forced. Our relationship was splintered—fractured by years of hurt, misunderstanding, and the weight of everything we endured. But healing has a way of working quietly, sometimes in the smallest moments. There are times now when we will wrap our arms around each other, holding on as if to make up for all the years we couldn't. In those embraces, my mom whispers the same powerful truth: "We made it out. We are free."

There were days when it felt like the pain would never end, like we were trapped in a cycle of suffering with no way forward. By God's grace, we are living proof that there is always a way through the heartache—that the grip of the past doesn't have to define the future. Freedom and peace come through breaking cycles, choosing truth, and refusing to stay bound by fear or guilt.

For years, I questioned my worth and carried labels that never belonged to me. Now I own my story and stand in it with strength. Healing took time, and unlearning took courage. But little by little, I've started to believe in myself. I'm learning to trust again. I've grown into someone I'm proud of. I love who God has formed through the fire. Others may have labeled me the black sheep, but I see now that I was a holy disruptor in the making.

If something in your life is robbing you of your peace, I encourage you to disrupt it. Challenge the patterns, break the chains, and step into a new way of living that will bring you true freedom—because on the other side of that fight, there is healing. And one day, you just may find yourself holding someone you love, whispering, "We made it out. We are free."

May the same stillness Jesus spoke over the storm rest over you and me.

Peace, be still.

Acknowledgments

To my personal Savior, Jesus Christ—Lord, thank you for giving me the strength to share my story. You are my constant peace, my Father, my redeemer. Without your love and grace, I wouldn't have the courage to face the truth of my past or the wisdom to know how to heal. Every word I write, every step I take, is a testament to your unending faithfulness in my life.

To my husband, Dillon—my best friend. Thank you for making me laugh when the weight of this journey felt unbearable, for asking the hard questions that pushed me to grow, and for believing in me when I couldn't believe in myself. You challenge me in ways no one else can. I'm forever grateful for the late-night talks, the silent prayers you've said for me, and the constant reassurance that keeps me moving forward. I choose you every single day.

To my son, Daxton—words can't express how much I love you. You are my little best friend. I wake up with joy in my heart every single day because you're mine. I will protect, nurture, and guide you with all that I am and all that I have, and I will always remind you of one truth: Mama and Daddy love you so much, but nobody loves you more than Jesus!

To my mom—I am so grateful that we have each other. Our

journey together, shaped by the trauma we've endured, has only made us stronger. I am in awe of your strength and how far you've come. Now we have each other, and nothing, not one single thing, can change that. Through every tear, every hardship, and every victory, we have stood by each other's side. Your healing has been my healing, and together we've created something unbreakable. Nothing can take that away from us, and for that I am endlessly thankful. I love you, and I always will.

To Susy Flory—thank you for shaping the structure of this book and for guarding my story with such care. Your support, guidance, and belief in this process were invaluable. It's been an honor to have you alongside me on this journey.

To Amy Butler—thank you for your undeniable way of seeing straight into my soul. You've always known exactly what to say, exactly when I needed to hear it. Your words have carried me through some of my hardest days and inspired me to rise with purpose. You've encouraged me to walk boldly like Deborah from the Bible—strong, wise, and unafraid to lead. You were the first to call me a *holy disruptor*, and those words lit a fire in me that I'll never forget. Because of you, I found the courage to write this book—and I pray it helps others rise up and become holy disruptors too.

To all the viewers who have supported me throughout the years—thank you. Your words of encouragement, your prayers, and the heartfelt messages you sent reached me in some of my darkest moments. When all I could hear were the lies of the Enemy, your voices reminded me of the truth. You spoke life over me when I felt unseen, and your kindness became a quiet strength that helped carry me through. You may never fully know how deeply your support has shaped the woman I am today. Your belief in me helped me keep going when I wanted to give up. For that I am forever grateful.

May this book meet you exactly where you are—in the middle of your healing, your questions, your rebuilding. And may it remind you that no matter what you've been through, you are never alone.

To the team at Zondervan—you protected my story. From start to finish, you honored the weight of my words and made sure my voice stayed true. It's been a privilege to work alongside people who lead with both excellence and heart. I don't believe it was by chance. God's hand has been on this book from the very beginning. Thank you for helping me tell this story the way it was meant to be told.

Notes

1. Kayla Aldecoa, "Jill Duggar Reveals Dad Jim Bob Made $8 Million from TLC: 'He'd Grown Rich Off the Show,'" *In Touch*, September 14, 2023, www.intouchweekly.com/posts /jill-duggar-reveals-how-much-money-jim-bob-made-from-tlc/.
2. William V. Mason, "The Crayon Box Song" (1972). Public domain.
3. "Duggar Cousin: Photo Extortion Plot Was 'Laughable,'" *Today*, February 27, 2012, www.today.com/video/duggar-cousin-photo-extortion -plot-was-laughable-44517955790.
4. *In Touch* Staff, "Bombshell Duggar Police Report: Jim Bob Duggar Didn't Report Son Josh's Alleged Sex Offenses For More Than a Year," *In Touch*, May 21, 2015, www.intouchweekly.com/posts /bombshell-duggar-police-report-jim-bob-duggar-didn-t-report-son -josh-s-alleged-sex-offenses-for-more-than-a-year-58906/.
5. Summary provided by Susy Flory.
6. Diana Chandler, "Josh Duggar Admits to Marital Infidelity," Baptist Press, August 20, 2015, www.baptistpress.com/resource-library/news /josh-duggar-admits-to-marital-infidelity/.
7. Summary provided by Susy Flory.
8. Teresa Roca, "Duggar Ex-Pals Jim and Bobye Holt Lose Custody of Kids and Are Deemed 'Unfit Parents' After 'Severe Physical and Mental Abuse,'" *U.S. Sun*, October 1, 2024, www.the-sun.com/entertainment /12570987/duggar-ex-pals-jim-bobye-holt-lose-custody-kids/.
9. Reid Nakamura, "Dr. Phil Discusses Josh Duggar Scandal on 'The View': 'For Every Rat You See, There's 50 You Don't,'" The Wrap, September 14, 2015, www.thewrap.com/dr-phil-discusses-josh-duggar-scandal-on-the -view-for-every-rat-you-see-theres-50-you-dont/.
10. Summary provided by Susy Flory.